HUMAN NATURE
HOW THE MIND GENERATES BEHAVIOR
Peter Bros

1998

INFORMATION
PHONE 1-703-971-9141
FAX 1-703-971-1628
info@copernican-series.com
http://www.copernican-series.com

PUBLISHED BY FINANCIAL BOOK PARTNERS
PRINTED IN THE UNITED STATES OF AMERICA
ISBN 0-9627769-9-8

Designed by Lemieux Creative Enterprises

HUMAN NATURE

HOW THE MIND GENERATES BEHAVIOR

Peter Bros

1. A REFLECTION OF THE MIND'S OPERATION 1
2. GOLDEN RULE BEHAVIOR 21
3. THINGS FOR WHICH WE CAN HAVE NO RECALL 39
4. THE UBIQUITOUS "I" 53
5. HOW SOCIETY PROGRAMS THE UBIQUITOUS "I" 69
6. THE EXERCISE OF FREE WILL 85
7. EXALTED EMPATHY 101
8. THE FAILURE TO PRODUCE ACCURATE TECHNOLOGY 119
9. COMMERCE 133
10. CONFLICT 147
11. THE NEED TO VIOLATE GOLDEN RULE BEHAVIOR 163
12. CONSUMED BY CHARITABLE IMPERATIVES 181
13. THE PATH TO SELF-DESTRUCTION 201

THE COPERNICAN SERIES

AT THE GATES OF THE CITADEL: THE SUBJUGATION OF MODERN SCIENCE

How the scientific method generates facts, conceptually blinding us to reality

THE COOLING CONTINUUM: THE RISE AND FALL OF SPECIES ON EARTH

How life forms and evolves and why it becomes extinct

ATOMS, STARS AND MINDS: SYNTHESIZING AN ELEMENTARY PARTICLE THAT COMPREHENDS ITSELF

How matter forms and moves in space

THE MODEL MIND: HOW THE MIND MOVES MATTER

How the mind is constructed and how it forms, stores and recalls images

HOW THE WEATHER <u>REALLY</u> WORKS!

What moves air masses, how they transport heat

LIGHT: REPLACING THREE CENTURIES OF MISCONCEPTIONS

Unifying light, heat, electricity and magnetism with a single concept

WHERE SCIENCE WENT WRONG: REPLACING FIVE CENTURIES OF MISCONCEPTIONS

The failure of science to deal with questions of force and motion

HUMAN NATURE: HOW THE MIND GENERATES BEHAVIOR

How society, technology and morality result from the mind's operation

FOR INFORMATION

PHONE 1-703-971-9141
FAX 1-703-971-1628
info@copernican-series.com
http://www.copernican-series.com

1. A REFLECTION OF THE MIND'S OPERATION

The institutions and the concepts of morality and law produced by our social interactions are simply reflections of the way our minds operate.

Because the purpose of the mind, the reason for which it evolved, is to act as a detector to move our bodies through physical reality, the mind operates to match what we see in reality with experience, what we have in recall. Recall is our experience encoded as pictures that are stored in the wet works of our brains, pictures which are available for comparison with what we see in reality. When our minds are merely doing what they evolved to do, when they are moving our bodies through physical reality, our recall function is forthright, dealing with actual physical reality.

Reality is made up of physical matter which can impede our movement through that reality. To be able to avoid these impediments, these obstacles to our movement through physical reality, we have to be able to recognize them as obstacles. The way we recognize something as an obstacle that needs to be avoided is to have encountered it before. To have encountered something before is to have formed a picture of it and to have stored that picture in our recall. As we subsequently move through reality for which we have recall, we can recall what we have seen and if what we have seen compares with what we see, if recall and reality agree, we can avoid the obstacles and continue to move freely through physical reality.

When our recall function is forthright, dealing with actual physical reality, we can always put the objects we see in reality in recall because the objects we see in reality are material objects, things, obstacles. As long as we can place pictures of the obstacles in reality in our recall, then when we see an obstacle we encounter in reality, we can recall pictures of how we have dealt with that obstacle in the past and we can move our bodies safely around the obstacle in physical reality.

When we have recall for the objects we see in physical reality, we comprehend, we understand what we see in reality because we can take effective action to deal with it.

However, when our minds evolve to the point that we can recall pictures of reality without reality being present, we can recall pictures of reality that are not apparent in reality. We become aware of things in reality which are not objects but which still require recall to understand.

We become aware of ourselves, we become aware of movement without apparent force, the movement of falling objects, and the movement of the sun and the moon, and we become aware of ourselves aware of movement without apparent force.

Thus, when we are using our recall to form pictures of reality, we have two separate realities for which we have to produce recall that will allow our minds to comprehend. We have to produce recall for things that are apparent, forthright, in reality and for things that are not apparent in reality.

With respect to the production of recall for things that are not apparent in reality, we have to produce recall for the movement of things in reality and for the existence of matter in reality, the universe and ourselves.

Further complicating the mind's operation once it can recall reality when reality is not present is it's ability to produce realities in recall that do not exist in reality. Instead of creating recall for realities, apparent or nonapparent, that actually exist in reality, the mind can produce recall for which there is no counterpart in reality.

We can create reality in recall about the physical objects in reality, and even about the movement of those objects in reality, and when we turn that recall into reality, we produce technology.

We also produce realities in recall that don't exist in reality as a result of the interactions that occur as we come together into societies. Because we act on recall whether or not that recall exists in reality, the recall of interactions in reality that don't exist in reality produce morality, a restraint on our behavior, on our movements in physical reality.

The structure of the mind evolved to deal with objects in reality, obstacles, objective facts. It did not evolve to deal with nonapparent reality, or with altering reality, or with restraining behavior in reality.

Before we can understand how our minds dictate the societies we construct, we first have to define the mechanisms the mind evolved to navigate forthright reality.

In order for our minds to move our bodies safely around obstacles in physical reality, the animate matter that makes us up had to develop a process that would allow us to recognize those obstacles. This process involves comparison, the comparison of what we are seeing with what we have already seen and stored in recall.

A process of comparison requires two sources for comparison and a place to carry out that comparison.

The first source of comparison is reality, the physical facts that exist in external reality, the outside world, the hard edges of physical reality. Reality exists independently of us. It is made up of inanimate objects. It is what we, as animate matter, have to navigate.

The second source of comparison is recall, the physical reality through which we have moved before and the pictures of which we have therefore stored in our recall. All of our knowledge of external reality comes from our senses which produce electrical representations of external reality. These electrical representations are stored in the wet works of our brains in such a way that when pictures of external reality are formed in our minds, recall stored in the wet works of our brain is brought into our minds for comparison with the representations that are already forming in our minds.

With two sources of comparison, there has to be a place for the comparison to occur.

We can picture the place in which the comparison process is carried out, the mind, as an electrical grid that holds a charge representing a particular condition in reality. When our senses transport charges to the grid, the resulting charge represents an objective picture of external reality.

Reality is filled with electromagnetic radiation made up of emission fields with specific frequencies.

Light is the most apparent of those frequencies.

Light allows us to know about reality. It allows us to navigate obstacles in physical reality by bouncing off of the hard edges of those obstacles.

Because light diminishes as it expands, and because it expands uniformly with distance, the amount of light at any point in its expansion, its presence, is mathematically measurable. Because the presence of light is mathematically measurable, light provides precise information about the relative locations of the physical objects in reality off which it bounces.

This is the information that, converted into electrical flows, the mind uses to form pictures of physical reality.

Because emission fields in reality are constantly changing and because we have to locate ourselves within those changing emission fields, the detector that evolved to move us through physical reality, our minds, had to develop a method that allowed our minds to store and recall representations of reality to compare with the reality streaming in from our senses.

The mind evolved to hold pictures of recall as electrical charges. As long as the electrical flows representing reality compare with the recalled electrical charges, we can proceed to move safely through external reality.

To reduce the process of electrical comparison to its simplest form, we can examine the primitive detectors that evolved to keep an organism out of hot water. Instead of detecting light bouncing off of the hard edges of physical reality, such a detector, a cluster of atoms, evolved to directly detect temperature. To detect temperature, a simple detector holds a range of charges that represents the survivable range of temperatures in which the organism can exist. As long as the cumulative charge in the environment in which the organism finds itself, the charge of the field representing temperature, compares to the range of charges the grid can maintain, the organism can remain quiescent in the environment.

However, if the temperature of the water increases, then the range of charges the electrical grid evolved to ensure the safety of the organism comes into conflict, no longer compares with the temperature and the detector reacts to the change in the environmental conditions. The detector that was quiescent when the temperature of the environment compared with the range of charges the detector holds now begins to actively dislodge some of the electrons of the atoms that make up the detector. The electrons become the electrical flows that signal the cilia that serve as paddles to move the organism. The cilia then begin to move until the organism has moved out of the hot water, the whole purpose of the mechanisms that evolved as detectors being to extend the range of survivability of the animate matter to which the detector is attached by allowing it to move safely with respect to the environment.

A cluster of atoms that merely detects temperature to allow an organism to stay out of hot water deals with forthright reality, the change in the water temperature of the environment in which the organism evolved.

A more complex strategy to extend an organism's range of survivability in physical reality is an electrical grid that can be programmed, much as applications program a computer's random-access memory. The electrical charge of the grid in such a mechanism remains neutral until it has a charge placed across it. Because of its neutrality, this electrical grid is capable of holding an infinite range of charges.

Carrying the computer analogy one step further, any set of charges that is placed in the random-access memory, the mind, by the electrical flows from the senses and which make up the representations of reality, can be stored as pictures in memory units similar to the genes we have conceptualized as programming the development of life. These memory units, instead of containing the blueprints for cell formation, contain simple pictures of physical reality.

In an organism with such a detector, pictures of physical reality will be transported to the electrical grid of the mind from the organism's senses. Once the electrical grid contains the charge that represents a picture of physical reality, the resulting electrical flows representing the picture of physical reality poll all of the stored memory units, the organism's experience, so that those that compare with the charge carried across the electrical grid can be recalled and tested against the charge across the grid, compared with the charge that represents the picture of physical reality.

If the recalled charge is compatible with the charge across the grid, we recall what we see and we comprehend.

Such a detector satisfies the need for a place where two sources representing reality can be compared. The electrical grid, the place for comparison, receives the electrical flows that represent reality from two sources, the pictures formed from reality and the pictures obtained from recall, and compare those pictures by their relative charges.

The comparison process occurs, our minds operate to produce comprehension, when recall and reality agree!

We only have one mind so that we can only form one picture at a time. Because the picture the mind forms comes from two source, the pictures both source provide have to agree, to compare.

While the simple detector evolved to merely move animate matter to more favorable climes when the environment changes, our minds are designed to allow us to make positive movements through physical reality, to act instead of react.

Our minds therefore evolved the comparison process to allow us to continue to move unless we encounter changed circumstances in physical reality!

We do not react to reality like an amoeba, we act positively in physical reality in order to move through that reality.

Any detector has to inform an organism about changes in physical reality. An organism that does not move through physical reality merely needs a detector that warns it when the conditions in reality have changed. It can remain quiescent in reality as long as the conditions in reality remain within its range of survivability.

We, on the other hand, need a detector that works in reverse. We have to move through physical reality to obtain our sustenance, not remain quiescent soaking up any sustenance that happens by.

When a detector only has to start movement when conditions in reality change, it merely has to have a template programmed into it that causes it to act when conditions change. The conditions that have to be avoided are known.

When an organism is moving through physical reality, the range of danger is infinite. The detector cannot be programmed against all dangers. It has to be programmed so that it can continue to move as long as reality is safe. The only way an organism could be programmed to know reality is safe is if the organism had safely navigated that reality and can recognize it as safe.

The simple detector is hard wired with the conditions that require movement.

The complex detector has to stop movement when conditions appear that endanger its existence!

To stop movement, the complex detector has to evolve a method to allow movement. To allow movement it has to allow the organism to form a picture of itself moving with respect to reality. To allow an organism to form a picture of itself moving with respect to reality requires that the organism be able to store pictures of itself moving with respect to reality. This is not difficult for an organism that evolved genetic units, the nonmeasurable blueprints that control the processes involved in the formation of organs and body parts.

Memory units, the genes of our recall, store information in the form of pictures rather than processes.

Once a mechanism evolved to store pictures of reality, an organism could move through reality so long as it had a picture of itself doing so.

And when the organism couldn't form a picture of itself moving through physical reality?

It could not move through physical reality!

Thus, if such an organism has a picture of itself moving though reality and that reality suddenly changes, the changes conflict with the pictures the organism is forming of itself moving through reality and the organism has to stop moving through reality until it can restart the recall process.

To move positively in physical reality, we have to have recall associated with that physical reality. We can't move if we don't have a picture of ourselves moving and we can't have a picture of ourselves moving unless we have been there before, trod the path, and have a picture of ourselves and the trodden path in recall.

Thus, when we move positively through physical reality, the only thing we need to know is if something in reality has changed from what we expect, what we have in recall.

Our minds, the detectors that evolved to allow us to move positively through physical reality, only need send us signals when we encounter something that has changed in physical reality.

Both simple and complex detectors evolved to notify the organism to which they are attached of changed circumstances, but the simple detector merely needs to get the organism moving if the environment changes, our hand reflexes when the burner gets hot, while our minds need to call our attention to changed circumstances, stop us before we step off the unexpected cliff into oblivion.

Continuing with the computer analogy, when our minds are programmed by reality, that reality sets up a serial recall process in which we recall the reality through which we are moving. Just like the computer, which operates so long as data conforms to instructions, as long as reality continues to agree with recall, our minds continue to function and we can move positively through that reality.

As long as our recall matches the picture of reality being formed from sensory input, the electrical grid, our mind, continues to operate and we can continue to move through reality without being startled by anything in that reality, without having our attention directed to potential dangers in reality.

Because such a mechanism would have evolved to move our bodies safely through external physical reality, as long as external physical reality does not present any dangers, our bodies can continue to move safely through that reality.

However, when reality forms a picture in our minds that interrupts our serial recall, then the comparison process ceases.

When we are walking down the familiar, well-trodden path, lost in our recall, and a ten foot spider suddenly drops down in front of us, we have no recall for the reality that is confronting us.

When this happens, with nothing to compare, our minds stop operating.

In spite of the quaint nineteenth century notion that our nerve impulses are the result of chemical interactions rather than electrical flows, when our minds stop operating, the electrical flows that operate our minds are still there. With nothing to do, they have to do something. With nowhere to go, they go into the wet works of our bodies, our subsystems, causing our bodies discomfort, pain.

This discomfort is the signal for our bodies to stop, and once stopped, for us to look around and find some sensory input that produces a template in our minds that we can use to poll our recall in an effort to produce an analogy, a comparison, an agreement, an understanding, comprehension of the big black hairy blob with its giant pincher legs bobbing in front of us so that we can once again get safely on our way. If we can't find recall that produces understanding, we might just blindly run, either into or away from danger, in the case of the spider, probably to the other side of the Earth. If we can find an analogy, produce understanding, we had one too many the night before and the spider is a product of our recall undergoing massive withdrawal, then we can once again move safely through physical reality.

When our minds are used for their evolved purpose, to move our bodies through physical reality, we are merely comprehending facts in physical reality. Our minds are merely forming pictures of something in reality, polling our recall to see if we can come up with something to compare with that picture, and if the polling is successful, we can move accordingly.

When we evolved so that our minds can recall reality without reality being present, however, our minds began to deal with things in reality which aren't objects and thus we began to use our minds for things that have nothing to do with their evolved purpose to move us safely through physical reality.

The difference between using our minds to dodge objects in reality and recall objects in reality when reality is not present is mirrored in the two levels of understanding involved with those objects.

Objects exist and objects move in existence.

We have little trouble recalling objects in order to move in relation to those objects.

But when we see objects move, when we see an object fall, we do not see what is making the object fall.

When reality is forthright, we can place the reality in recall so that when we later encounter the reality, we can recall what we see and our minds can continue to operate.

However, when reality is not forthright, when we are dealing with the movement of objects in reality, we are faced with a reality that is present for which we have no recall, and nothing apparent to put in recall.

When we see an object move in reality, we can touch the object but we can't touch what is making it move. We can recall the object but we can't recall why the object is moving.

When we see movement in reality, we don't have anything in recall with which we can compare with reality!

If we have not evolved to the point that we can recall reality when reality is not present, we do not have a problem with recall dealing with what makes objects fall, we just produce recall of falling objects that allows us to avoid having them fall on our heads.

But when we evolve to the point that we can recall reality when reality is not present, then we have the time to closely examine the recall of that reality and recall that is not apparent becomes apparent.

We find that we have no recall for the reality we are recalling.

When we are moving through physical reality, and encounter something that doesn't match our recall, our minds stop operating because we have nothing in recall to compare with reality. We receive a shock from the electrical flows that were operating our minds and which now direct our attention to the changes in physical reality which will produce a recall that will result in comparison and get our minds operating so that we can once again move through physical reality.

It is the failure to compare that stops our minds from operating.

When we see something about objects in reality that isn't apparent in reality, we have the same problem we have when we see objects in reality for which we have no recall. Our minds stop operating because they have nothing to compare with reality.

When our minds stop operating, we feel discomfort in our bodies.

Because we don't want to feel discomfort in our bodies, because we don't want to feel pain, because we want to get out of the situation of having pain, we are driven to put something in recall that agrees with what we see in reality.

The need to make up recall to match nonapparent reality in order to avoid the pain that results when the mind cannot perform its evolved function of matching recall and reality controls how we construct the institutions and concepts of morality and law that then govern our interactions with one another.

On an elementary level, the mind is simply an electrical grid that holds a charge that represents reality. Memory units are stored in the wet works of the brain. These memory units are recalled to match the electrical charge reality produces on the grid. When we see a tree in physical reality, we recall a tree because the electrical charge the tree produces on the grid matches the electrical charge of the memory units located in the wet works of the brain that contain pictures of trees and the memory units holding the picture of trees are carried to the grid for comparison with the representation of the tree formed by the grid.

When we see a tree we recall a tree and we comprehend what we see, we see a tree and we understand that it is a tree.

It is the fact of comparison, the agreement of recall and reality that produces comprehension, that gives us the sense of having meaning in what we see.

However, when we see a tree and we have nothing in recall to match the tree, we feel a discomfort that drives us to figure out what we are seeing.

I call the things for which we have no recall purple flimgasts.

When we see a tool whose function puzzles us, a tool for which we have no recall, we keep looking at it at different angles. We hold it up to the light and look at it first this way, and then that, in an attempt to puzzle out its utility.

Moving the hard edges of the reality that make up the tool changes the light bouncing off of the tool and alters the level of the electrical flows moving through the wet works of our brain. We are varying the electrical flows in an attempt to recall a picture that will produce understanding. We keep this up until we produce an electrical flow that will recall something that will allow us to use recall to match the reality we see.

If we can't figure out what the tool is for, we produce a category in which to place the things for which we have no recall, purple flimgasts, so that every time we see the mysterious tool we can recall that it is a purple flimgast, something that totally puzzles us, and we will feel no pain because we will have simulated comprehension for what we see.

When we see things for which we have no recall, we make up something to put in our recall so that we will have the feeling of understanding.

We make up recall to avoid the pain of not comprehending what we see!

It doesn't matter what we make up so long as we don't produce a picture that contains elements for which we have no recall. We don't want to answer a question by creating more questions, we just want to get out of the pain of seeing something for which we have no recall.

Thus, when we see an object fall, we know what the object is, we have in recall that if the object falls on us, it will kill us, so we know to get out from under falling objects, but we have no recall for what is making the object fall. As we become aware of our ability to form pictures of reality when reality is not present, we will form pictures of falling objects in our recall when reality is not present. However, the hole in our recall will become apparent as we examine the pictures of falling objects in our recall.

We will not be able to recall what is making the objects fall and, unless we come up with some recall to fill the hole, we will feel pain.

Purple flimgasts won't do for falling objects because falling objects are pervasive, always present. If we don't hold ourselves up against the invisible force that makes objects fall, we will ourselves become falling objects!

We have to make up something that makes us believe that we actually know what is making the object fall, so we make up gravity, say it is a property of mass, and when we see falling objects, we can recall words that make us believe we comprehend what we see and we feel no pain.

Of course gravity is just another purple flimgast, a category into which we place only one thing for which we have no comprehension.

The word gravity doesn't explain anything about how objects fall.

That's why we have to source what we make up in the occult, that gravity is a property of matter. Properties just exist, they are the mysteries, the purple flimgasts of nature.

The inability to produce recall for the reality of our existence is, like the inability to produce recall for the source of movement in physical reality, a product of our having evolved to the point where we can recall reality when reality is not present. When we recall pictures of reality when reality is not present, we can form a picture of ourselves in reality.

We look at ourselves in recall and ask, where did we come from?

The resulting hole in our picture of reality, the source of our existence in reality, becomes apparent because, not having physical counterparts in reality, the nonapparent source of our existence is not forthright, not an object, not an obstacle in reality. Unable to produce recall for our existence, the resulting inability to compare causes us pain which draws our attention to the lack of recall and thus the hole in our recall.

Just as with falling objects, where the object is a reality and the motion a mystery, our existence is a fact, we exist, and our source, where we came from, an unknown!

Just as we are driven to make up recall to explain the nonapparent motions in nature, so too are we driven to make up recall to explain our existence, and the existence of the world, all the life upon it, and the universe around it.

If we don't make up something to put in our recall that matches the things in reality for which we have no recall, then we are in pain. The only way we can get out of pain is to make up something to put in recall.

We create religious systems.

When it comes to comprehending things that are not objects in reality, that are not forthright, the need to make up recall to match reality drives us to produce occult systems like mass/gravity, or religious systems to avoid the pain that not knowing, not having recall, produces.

So we have objects in reality, falling objects and ourselves in physical reality, and we have mysteries involving those objects in reality, what makes objects fall and how we got here.

What we make up about how we got here is a matter of personal preference and will not affect how well we can survive independent of the environment. What we make up about movement and the source of force has everything to do with whether we can extend our range of survivability in physical reality!

While objects in physical reality can always be measured, the nonapparent source of motion and existence can never be measured. We can never know what makes objects fall, and we can never know how the matter that makes us up came into existence. We can only make up stuff and put it into our recall. The pain of not knowing drives us to do so, to create made-up stuff we can put in recall so that we will have something to compare with the realities producing the puzzle to avoid the pain produced by not having recall that matches reality.

We can make up stuff which, when placed in recall, makes us believe we are recalling reality because the comparison process occurs in the mind which only produces a representation of realty and not reality itself.

Even when the reality that we are dealing with is forthright, the mere recall of an object we have seen in reality and stored in recall for later comparison, the recall is identical to the recall of the stuff we make up because we judge the validity of recall by whether it compares with the pictures we have in our minds, not whether the comparison deals with reality.

Once we reconstruct a picture of a rock from seeing a rock in reality, the representation of the rock in our minds is no more real than the rock we reconstruct in our minds from recall. Because it is only recall that gives the pictures in our minds meaning when the recall matches those pictures, we obtain our meaning from recall.

When reality is forthright, we can force the picture in our mind to match the picture of reality by measurement.

When reality is forthright, measurement keeps us honest!

When reality is not apparent, when there is no object in reality, when we are dealing with force, the cause of motion, or the source of our existence, then what we make up to put in our recall to match the nonapparent reality becomes more real than reality itself because there is nothing in reality to contradict it, nothing to measure.

When we are dealing with reality that is forthright, we can bump into it and we hurt.

When we are dealing with nonapparent reality, the source of the force that makes objects fall or the source of the matter that makes us up, there is nothing to bump into.

We can believe what we like because it can never be contradicted by reality.

When we can produce a picture of reality without reality being present, we can focus on specific elements of the picture and, by altering current levels in much the way we alter them when we puzzle over purple flimgasts, we can alter the specific elements of the picture. Because we each have only one mind, and can form only a single picture of reality at any one time, altering the elements of a picture serves to alter the entire picture causing new pictures to emerge, pictures that do not exist in physical reality.

This is creativity.

Creativity is how we use the mind, the ultimate tool of evolution, to extend our range of survivability in physical reality.

When we form pictures of physical reality that do not exist in physical reality, we have produced a reversal of the comparison process the mind evolved to move the body safely through physical reality.

Our minds operate by comparing reality with recall and when something in reality does not match the recall reality has evoked, our minds stop operating and send the electrical flows that were operating them into our subsystems as *neuronic impacts* in order to shock us into paying attention to reality rather than recall.

Once the process of moving through reality starts the recall process, it is the recall process that we see. When we see something in physical reality we do not have in recall, we receive a start, a burst of electrical current that causes us discomfort.

These unwanted electrical flows, the result of our mind's failure to operate, are called neuronic impacts because the mind is chemically attached to the wet works of our brains and the wet works of the brain is made up of neurons.

These neuronic impacts cause us to focus our attention on what it is about physical reality that doesn't match our recall process.

When the reverse occurs, when we have constructed a house in our mind, and that house doesn't exist in reality, then every time we see reality without the house, we are subjected to the same neuronic impacts that occur when we are moving through reality and reality doesn't agree with recall. The failure of reality to compare with recall in this case drives us to change reality so that it matches recall.

We then go out and attempt to create our recall in reality.

When the pictures of altered reality we make up deal with forthright reality, with objects in reality, we can test reality to determine if we can turn our made-up reality into physical reality.

This leads to technology.

Technology is the process of changing the environment to make it more conducive to our survival, the mind being the tool we use to reverse the process of evolution in which the environment dictates the shape life takes. When life is dictated by the environment, it is dependent on the environment. Nonambulatory trees cannot flee a forest fire. However, when life can choose the environment, flee the forest fire, or change the environment, extinguish the forest fire, then it can extend its range of survivability in that environment.

The extent to which we become independent of the environment controls the extent to which we can survive independent of that environment.

Making mistakes of meaning, mistaking recall dealing with nonapparent reality with recall about facts will retard technology and limit our range of survivability within the environment. The trial and error process empirical science claims as its basic tool for understanding physical reality is actually the tool of technology. We produce a recall that doesn't exist, and then test reality to see if the recall can in fact exist in reality. The facts in reality shape the nature of the recall we make up to envision changes in that reality.

However, if we make up a bunch of silly stuff, occult explanations for how reality works, properties, like gravity, that cause movement, angular momentum in closed systems for why the planet rotates, swirling masses of gas for planetary rotation, moving charges for electricity, molecular magnets for magnetism, or waves for light, and then mistake those occult concepts for facts, the recall we create in our attempt to extend our range of survivability in physical reality will never produce elements of a picture that will allow us to actually change physical reality because the elements that we are trying to change, which are taken as fact, are merely silliness, chimera, nonexistence.

If we think the most significant force in our existence, the force that holds us to the surface of the Earth, gravity, is an occult property that simply exists, then when we attempt to alter reality with respect to that force, we will never attempt to form pictures of a technology that uses gravity as a current, physical mechanism, instead producing a technology that mimics the fishes, contraptions that glide through air like fishes move through water.

Instead of extending our range of survivability, mistaking concepts for facts will put us to sleep with the fishes we so ardently attempt to imitate.

While the conflict of recall with reality, and the resulting neuronic impacts, drives us to alter physical reality to match the pictures we form, if we are totally confused about what are facts, and what is made-up stuff put in our recall to stop neuronic impacts, our failure to distinguish our fantasies from fact will keep us from extending our range of survivability within the environment.

We will revert to the fate of the mindless, devolve to disaster as once again the environment controls our destiny.

If we can't see reality, we can't alter it to extend our range of survivability within that reality. How we answer the questions underlying the technology our minds are driven to create will determine the extent to which we can extend our range of survivability in physical reality, determine whether we, in fact, will survive.

If we form a picture of a physical reality that doesn't exist in reality, we might form a picture of a house instead of a cave and shelter ourselves from the environment. On the other hand, forming a picture in recall of a reality that doesn't exist can also lead us to form pictures in our recall that deal with others in physical reality.

We might form a picture of a physical reality in recall that would exist in reality but for the fact that we are not a part of that physical reality. We might, depending on sex, form a picture of the ruby on our neighbor's wife's finger on our finger, or a picture of us on our neighbor's wife.

In this case, instead of leading to technology, our ability to form pictures of a reality in recall when reality is not present leads to morality.

Because the neuronic impacts that drive us to create our concepts of morality do not involve physical reality, they are akin to our conclusions dealing with nonapparent reality. They are not limited by the feedback manipulating objects in physical reality produces.

While picturing a changed physical reality that produces technology and picturing a changed physical reality that puts us in another's position have a common basis by driving us to create a reality that matches recall, the questions underlying morality are based on the need for people to come together and live together in a society. When we are treated to a picture of objective physical reality that does not include ourselves, our neighbor's wife with a sparkling ring, our sparkling neighbor's wife, the neuronic impacts that result from our recall not matching reality drives us to make our recall a reality. We are not in the picture but we can easily substitute ourselves as an element in the picture.

When we put ourselves in a picture of physical reality that does not match the picture of physical reality that exists in physical reality, we have produced a picture of recall that doesn't agree with reality.

The mind is incapable of forming two opposing pictures at the same time. As a result, the mind stops operating to the extent that we put ourselves in a picture of reality that doesn't exist in reality and the resulting neuronic impacts drive us to put ourselves in the picture.

We steal our neighbor's wife's ring or mount our neighbor's wife.

When our actions in physical reality affect others in physical reality, we create recall that drives others to act in physical reality.

Recall dealing with objects in physical reality is forthright and merely allows us to navigate physical reality successfully.

Recall about the nonapparent cause of motion, or the nonapparent source of our existence merely drives us to make up recall that doesn't disagree with what we see.

When we are producing realities that don't exist based on the objective interactions of physical matter, how it can be arranged to produce more beneficial relationships, we produce objective technology that then becomes a forthright part of physical reality.

However, when we produce realities based on our interactions with others in physical reality, we are dealing with subjective relationships, and subjective relationships may well produce recall that drives others to act in specific, and not particularly pleasant ways.

There is no more solid picture of physical reality than our relationship to the objects that we possess in physical reality.

Thus, when we create recall of ourselves possessing that which others have and then act on that recall in order to avoid the neuronic impacts the recall produces, we are putting ourselves in possession of something that is already possessed by someone else.

The neuronic impacts that drive us to take another's possessions are nothing when compared to the neuronic impacts caused in those whose possessions we take.

In our fantasy involving our neighbor's wife, and I use neighbor's wife because it is basic biblical, and thus societal, morality, the wife has a recall that contains a picture of herself inviolate with ring intact.

When we alter reality by putting ourselves in the picture, we have created conflicting pictures in the minds of our victims and set off cascades of neuronic impacts.

Neuronic impacts are the result of the electricity that operates the mind entering the physical subsystems of the body. The unwanted electricity disrupts those subsystems causing pain, heart attacks, stomach cramps, headaches, sweating, involuntary bowel movements, the entire panoply of physical ailments.

Physical acts in physical reality leave tracks in that physical reality because they produce recall which exists independent of reality. Because acts are events in physical reality, they become, much the same as objects in physical reality, a part of recall and are recallable regardless of what exists in physical reality.

Transgressions against our neighbor's wife can never be undone because having occurred in physical reality, they have become a part of the recall of the participants.

One way to get rid of the excess electricity produced by neuronic impacts is to engage in physical activity. The operation of the muscles generates heat which dissipates the electricity as heat into the surrounding air.

Thus, one way our neighbor's wife could respond to the neuronic impacts produced by our acts would be to use muscle power to eliminate the source of the pain.

If the she doesn't kill us, her husband will.

Another way our neighbor's wife could get rid of the neuronic impacts is to have an objective third party extract redress from us.

Much of the morality produced by religious systems and the law produced by civil systems involve addressing acts that leave neuronic impacts behind by creating adequate redress for transgressions that have altered the recall of the participants forever.

Why is it important to address redress?

Every time a victim recalls a wrong, he is subjected to the same neuronic impacts that he received during the original event. As long as he can recall the event, he is driven to retaliate. The physical effect can outlast the death of the instigator because it is the recall of the event that is producing the neuronic impacts.

We have an interest in addressing redress because redress, revenge if you will, blunts our recall, makes it less painful.

But if the redress itself produces recall that in turn requires revenge, the cycle would become never ending.

The process of addressing redress produces the morality that underlies societal interactions by restraining us from acting in response to our own neuronic impacts in ways that would cause others neuronic impacts.

The ability to create a reality in recall that does not exist in reality produces, as a result of the mind's operation, neuronic impacts that drive us to turn our recall into reality. When the recall we manufacture involves taking the property of another or otherwise infringes on another person's recall, then we have created a conflict of recall with reality in that person that produces neuronic impacts that drive that person to retaliate.

We cannot live together if we are continually driven by neuronic impacts to retaliate.

The morality we create is driven by the need to eliminate neuronic impacts.

Our institutions and our concepts of morality and law reflect the mind's operation by restraining our behavior and thereby reducing the neuronic impacts in society so that society can exist.

2. GOLDEN RULE BEHAVIOR

We know that the pain that drives behavior exists because we can feel it. Thoughts can devastate us, make us sick, kill us.

But the mind does not show up in photographs and it can't be X-rayed.

Although the mind can be broken and it can break us, we deny its existence because empiricists have not been able to excise it and put it on the shelf between the bottled livers and pancreatic juices.

We can only measure the mind by its effect which, of course, is precisely what empiricists do with force.

Gravity is not something we can store in a bottle. We can only determine its existence by the way it makes objects drop on Earth. Magnetism and light do not lend themselves to bottled display. And the electron which is used to explain electricity is neither here nor there according to the quantum principles espoused by empiricists, even though it lights our nights.

While the electron is hypothetical, it clearly exists. It produces electrical flows. And no matter how hypothetical empiricists consider the mind, they couldn't hold their rulers to reality without it.

Because we measure electrical flows at work in the wet works of the brain, we can make a pretty safe claim that electrons in the form of electrical flows generate the mind.

If we view the mind as we view the structure of matter, as particles held together in webs of stable equilibrium, we can visualize how electrical flows might produce representations of reality in such a structure. Matter is thought to be made up of atoms held together by electrical charges of one sort or another, and the mind, composed of electrons, can also be visualized as held together by electrical charges.

Instead of visualizing an amorphous electrical grid, we can picture ten rows of ten electrons, one hundred evenly spaced dots on a plane multiplied by ten planes of a hundred dots so that each plane is evenly spaced to make a cube of one thousand evenly spaced dots. Although the mind is made up of uncountable electrons, our hypothetical cube of one thousand evenly spaced electrons can be used to demonstrate how the mind forms representations of physical reality.

The grid of electrons is held together in a stable web of electrical equilibrium.

When an electrical flow passes through the grid, it disturbs the equilibrium of the grid and the individual electrons move out of their positions of stable equilibrium.

The movement of the electrons making up the grid from their positions of stable equilibrium register as a representation of physical reality.

The extent to which the current level disbalances the electrons that make up the grid is proportional to the level of the flows. Because the light that bounces off of each of the hard edges of reality has a different presence, a different level of flow, and because the conversion of light to electrical flows in the wet works of the brain is proportional to that presence, the information about the hard edges of the objects in physical reality can be transported through the wet works of the brain and duplicated across the electrical grid.

With the strength of the emission flows of light representing reality affecting the stable equilibrium of our minds in proportion to their presence, we all form objective representations of reality in our minds so that when we see a tree, we all see representations of the same hard edges in reality, the same tree.

With the mind being made up of electrons, it is only detectable by the electrical flows that operate it. With the grid held into place chemically by the wet works of the brain, the mind is electrically absorbed into the environment when those wet works cease to function.

However, just because we can't cut it out and toss it in the waste bucket doesn't mean we can't measure it and physically analyze its function.

We can measure the mind by what happens to the electrical flows that operate it when the mind stops operating!

The viewpoint of empirical science, which requires acceptable interpretations of facts before those facts empirically exist, is that the mind does not exist, that without the mind there can be no mind/body connection, and that neuronic impacts therefore don't exist, that nerve impulses travel like slow light waves, as disturbances of the nerve rather than as something that moves through the nerve itself. Empirical science, in fact, with its quantum belief that matter does not exist until it is observed, is perilously close to the conclusion that, without the existence of the mind, matter itself doesn't exist.

With respect to the electrical flows in the wet works of the brain which are easily measurable by the most primitive of technologies, empirical science considers electricity to be a moving charge which has no existence outside of its measurement. Because moving charges need a force to move them, and because empirical science has no way to understand force, it uses an analogy to magnets to explain the movement of the electrons that it hypothesizes make up flows of electricity. Empirical science has no idea why a magnet moves with respect to another magnet, but by labeling one side positive and the other side negative, it creates a series of words, opposites attract, that we can put in recall and therefore simulate understanding of the force when we see something move with no apparent force.

With "opposites attract" in recall, when we see two magnets move, we recall that opposites attract, and we believe we understand the movement.

When we see generated electricity do work at a distance, we apply the same recall, opposites attract, to explain why the electricity is moving even though it is moving in a circuit and even though there are no opposite charges to attract.

With the concept of electricity as a moving charge, we can form a picture of the electricity that operates the mind as something that moves from one place to another without the need for concepts of polarity, of positive or negative, and with the accepted picture of electricity jumping the conceptual synapses between neurons, we can form a picture of electricity as something that flows through the pathways of the body.

The concept that blocks the general acceptance of electrical flows moving from the mind to the body's subsystems through the pathways of the nervous system is the misapplication of the concept of positive and negative to explain why electricity flows. Because the brain is not negative and the subsystems are not positive, electricity cannot flow from one to the other.

It is easier to maintain the misapplication of positive and negative and create an occult concept of opposite charges undulating down the surface of the nerve like a slinky down a staircase, a concept with no basis in reality, than to try to actually understand how electricity works.

Electricity, however, like light, which speeds back up after it is slowed down, is energy, with the movement of the particles that make it up a property of the particle itself.

Therefore, electricity doesn't need something to cause it to move, it just needs a place towards where it can move.

If we disconnect the law of opposites attracting that was codified by watching magnetic dogs kiss from contemplation about the subatomic world, and specifically to electricity as likes repelling, we can get rid of a whole bunch of particles that were made up to explain physical effects because, locked into the assumption that opposites attract is the belief that there has to be something opposite there to do the attracting.

Without the need for opposites attracting, and thus no requirement that likes repel, electrons can merely attract and a flow of electricity move to where there is a deficit of electrons.

Electrical currents course through the mind without benefit of a circuit, without the inappropriate application of an analogy to positive or negative and even without a source for their generation.

It would therefore appear to be eminently acceptable to conclude that, with no source of generation, and no need for a negative analogy, that electrical currents do what they do, invade the wet works of the body when the mind stops operating. After all, we can put electrodes on our heads that will allow us to move cursors on a computer screen. When we take a lie detector test, and we lie, which is to say we create a picture in recall that we know didn't occur in reality, the failure to compare at the basis of the lie stops our minds from operating and the electrical flows that were operating them enter our bodies and measurably evidence themselves as an increased heart beat, sweating palms and more rapid breathing.

Even if empirical science could accept the existence of the mind, however, it could not accept the fact that electrical flows move from the brain to the body because, in the nineteenth century, when it was thought that electricity flowed on the outside of a conductor, empirical science conclusively concluded that there was no electricity flowing on the outside of the nerves connecting the mind to the body.

If electricity didn't travel on the outside of the nerve, and it couldn't travel within the wet works of the nerve itself, it must not travel at all. Nerves, then, must have some other way to transmit signals.

What could be more logical, empiricists ruled, than to have nerve impulses travel like light, which, according to empirical lights, has no independent existence.

If the inside and outside of a nerve had equal and opposite charges until something touched the nerve, then, empiricists exclaimed, when the nerve is touched, the charge will be disturbed. When the equal charge is disturbed, contiguous charges will also be disturbed in a cascade of motionless movement. In a manner whose mechanics eludes the ever attentive acolytes of empirical science, *and because according to the empirical process, what could be, is,* this disturbance, like the waves passing through a slinky, cascades down the nerve with its message of movement.

However, no electrical flows are moving.

Empirical science's explanation for all that goes on within us, then, is that nothing goes on within us!

If we see something in reality that startles us, ancient reptilian programming dictates that we fight or flight from the fright, and the body produces substances like adrenalin that allows us to do so, and any feeling we have in our body is the result of the adrenalin, not of electrical flows moving from the mind to the body which might need damping by the adrenalin.

We end up with the rather ridiculous picture of a learned body of knowledge telling us we evolved all of these marvelous subsystems, but that everything we evolved is nonfunctional, that there is nothing behind our eyes receiving information from the environment, that the pictures we form are made up of chance connections of the cells that make up our brains, neurons, that the place where the pictures are formed, where we evaluate what is going on in reality and make choices about what to do in that reality doesn't exist, and therefore doesn't communicate with our subsystems, the arms and legs that evolved to move us through that reality, that our minds, nonexistent, do not communicate with the hands that fashion the technology our minds create, that the picture of our neighbor stealing our spouse is nothing at all, just a primitive territorial instinct that results in mindless reaction, that really, this superb integration of subsystems that moves us through reality and allows us to alter reality to our benefit, is just some dumb show with no basic mechanical explanation.

The anger we feel when someone blocks our rightful path, cuts us off in the car or throws us the bird, the wrath we feel when we remember someone blocking our rightful path, cutting us off in the car or throwing us the bird, the fury we feel when we imagine someone blocking our rightful path, cutting us off in the car or throwing us the bird, the uncontrollable rage we can work ourselves into without reference to reality should be sufficient to make us realize that something physical is going on, that the mind is something physical, the body is something physical, the brain operates on the basis of electricity and thus the mind is electrically based, and that the electricity that operates the mind is the electricity that is producing the pain that sends the mind into retreat and the body into paroxysms of rage.

The unneeded electrical flows flood our subsystems which have no use for them and we feel pain!

Because electrons normally move to where there is a deficit of electrons, and because there are no unsatisfied deficits of electrons when our bodies are moving freely through physical reality, the movement of the electrons in the form of neuronic impacts disrupts the normal operations of our subsystems which are themselves operating as a result of electrons moving back and forth among the deficits created in them by our relationship to, and movement through physical reality.

The various emotions that we experience are the subjective interpretations of these neuronic impacts.

If we feel neuronic impacts associated with specific actions that harmed us, we interpret the pain as anger. If we are thwarted in our attempts to revenge the pain of our anger, we interpret the neuronic impacts as frustration. If we succeed in our revenge, if we wreak vengeance on our tormentor, we feel no neuronic impacts and interpret their absence as joy. If we wreaked vengeance on the wrong party, or if we have second thoughts about our actions after we have left our bloody tracks in reality, we interpret the neuronic impacts as remorse.

If we feel neuronic impacts associated with the recall of actions that we have engaged in, actions which we wish we hadn't engaged in, we interpret the pain as guilt.

However we interpret the neuronic impacts, though, they are the same neuronic impacts caused by the same failure of comparison.

While it is difficult to visualize the mind's operation by exception, that to operate, to perform its function, it has to stop operating, it is not difficult to track the pain that results when it stops operating, when we are presented with opposing pictures of reality.

Opposing pictures of reality, where reality doesn't agree with our recall, produce neuronic impacts which call our attention to changed reality so we can continue to move safely through that reality.

In their normal operation, our minds receive a picture of reality in the form of electrical flows that represent that reality. Those electrical flows reflect the elements of the picture formed, and once the picture is formed, the picture establishes an electrical flow at a specific frequency with a particular charge. The flows bearing this particular charge move throughout the wet works of our brains, our neurons, in order to pick up memory units with similar charges so that what has been formed in our minds and stored in our neurons can be recalled for comparison with what is being formed in our minds.

Once reality produces recall, we focus on recall, with serial recall, the moving pictures that are connected by the similar charges at which related pictures are stored in our neuronic storage bins, the wet works of our brains, allowing us to conform our bodies to our pictures of recall as we move physically through reality.

Reality is continually evoking recall, but it is the serial recall that is evoked by reality that allows us to move safely through physical reality.

When a picture from reality does not agree with the serial recall reality is evoking, our minds stop operating and the electricity, with nowhere to go, enters the wet works of our bodies, our brains, our hearts, our stomachs, our bowels, disrupting their operations and thus calling attention to the conflict in our minds, the changes in reality that need our attention.

But, if there is no reality present, if we are operating on the basis of recall alone, how does the conflict that produces neuronic impacts arise?

How can we will ourselves into a rage when there is no reality present?

In *The Model Mind* I focused on how the mind moves matter, the matter being the body, but, in addition I delved deeply into the revenge triggered by imagined transgressions. In doing so, I set up two "I"s that are continuously operating in the mind.

One "I" is the intellectual "I".

The intellectual "I" is the self that is generated by the continuous recall operation of the mind. Every picture of reality that we form and store in recall contains the point of view of the self. The picture of the self is always recalled as a part of all recall formed in the mind.

We eventually become aware of this self.

Being aware of ourselves being aware is the advanced level of evolution described in the last chapter, the result of being able to hold pictures of reality in recall when reality is not present. It is this self, the result of the series of pictures being recalled at any particular time, that makes up the intellectual "I" that is a part of all recall in the mind.

Our intellectual "I", our concept of self, is relatively stable from second to second because every picture we recall has a picture of ourself as a part of that picture.

However, we store pictures at a particular current level that exists at the time we are experiencing the events that make up the pictures.

All pictures of our self are therefore stored at charges related to the current levels associated with the events we were experiencing when the pictures were stored as memory units.

This allows us to compartmentalize our lives, with the recall associated with work producing an intellectual "I" that is comfortable in the office, the recall that is associated with family producing an intellectual "I" that is comfortable at home, a social intellectual "I" that goes to parties, even a sick intellectual "I" that gets us through the flu.

Sex forever fascinates us because when we experience sex, we are storing the recall of the sexual act at a unique current level totally inaccessible when we are going about our everyday lives. In the light of day, our sexual experiences might as well have occurred to aliens on the other side of the moon, and we only risk dwelling on them when we are in a position to duplicate them because once recalled, our sexual intellectual "I"s are in recall and in control of our bodies.

Our minds always generate an intellectual "I" when we are recalling, when we are in a state of awareness, of consciousness.

However, there is another "I" that is always being generated by recall. This second "I" is based on the evolved purpose of the mind as a detector.

The purpose of recall is to move the body through physical reality, not to produce a self that can contemplate the universe so that all recall has a picture of the body with its location in physical reality as a necessary component.

In The Model Mind I styled this recall generated self the external "I".

If we are lying in bed contemplating our future, and we begin to dwell on our relationship with our boss and coworkers, we could well sigh, conclude everything was all right, and go to sleep with a rosy picture of the future in our minds.

Or we could envision the blackguard that sits behind us sneaking into the coffee room after everyone has gone home and peeing in the coffee pot!

Why, the thought is enough to start steam rising from our forehead. How could that dastard do such a thing?

We picture our external "I" going to the coffee urn, unknowingly pouring a cup of coffee, taking it back to our desk, and taking a sip. Does it taste sour? Does it taste bitter? This is the bastard that probably went into the boss's office yesterday just before we got that awful assignment to determine how many thumbtacks can be saved by locking the bulletin board. We can picture the conversation that occurred. The boss wanted the idiot that's pissing in the coffee pot to take the tacky assignment but being a clever nitwit, he suggested us, and now we have to drink piss and count thumb tacks . . .

We could, in the darkness of a night that provides no limit to our range of recall, go on and on like this, keeping ourselves awake all night and into the wee hours of the morning, our stomachs churning, our hearts pounding, even our heads aching as wave after wave of electricity flowed unwanted into our subsystems.

The question we are here asking is, without a reality present, how can we have a conflict with reality, and the answer is, we are recalling a picture of ourselves in external reality reacting to events with a basis in reality but existing only in our recall.

We are seeing ourselves wronged.

Our external "I"s are being observed by our intellectual "I"s, the "I"s that have certain standards of conduct at the core of their self, in this case the standard of a positive external "I" treated decently in physical reality, and every time our external "I"s experience something that conflicts with the core standards set up by our intellectual "I"s, the positive image of self our intellectual "I"s need for us to move through physical reality, our minds are being forced to form two pictures at the same time, a picture of made-up reality that opposes our idealistic picture of reality that makes up the self that is our intellectual "I".

In the arena of recall there is no question of right and wrong.

Our intellectual "I"s are the "I"s that we live with day in and day out. We all have to have a positive intellectual "I" in order to form the pictures of our external "I" that are necessary for us to act in reality. In order to move in external reality we have to be able to picture ourselves moving in external reality.

The process of moving across a room requires that we first form a positive picture of our external "I" on the other side of the room.

"Positive" means that we can form a picture in recall that doesn't exist in reality while enduring the neuronic impacts that the resulting conflict with reality produces.

Actually moving across the room involves turning our recall into reality. Our recall knows at every instant where every part of our external "I" is located in reality so that moving across the room merely entails conforming our body parts to the pictures of our body in recall as it makes the physical motions required to move. At each point of the movement our recall is slightly ahead of our motion in physical reality unless we have been overcome by the neuronic impacts, having formed a picture of ourselves in recall moving faster than we can in reality, in which case we might stumble over our own feet, or over someone else's.

If we couldn't summon up a positive picture of ourselves acting in physical reality, we would stay motionless and blend into the wallpaper.

But whether we are overeager to reach our destination, or reluctant to meet our fate, without a positive picture of ourselves acting in reality, we cannot act!

Unless we have abdicated our actions to another by agreeing to play follow the leader or deciding to allow others to act upon our passive body, the intellectual "I" that is in our recall has to have a positive picture of our external "I" acting in our recall or we simply cannot act.

When we visualize our external "I"s being mistreated in recall, that mistreatment conflicts with our positive intellectual "I"s and neuronic impacts result.

Of course, if our intellectual "I"s are accustomed to being kicked around, if the concept of self that we have evolved is a result of mistreatment, constant harassment or condescension, then forming pictures of our external "I"s being mistreated might agree with our intellectual "I"s and we might take pleasure in the imagined mistreatment. In fact, if our intellectual "I"s are accustomed to mistreatment, fair treatment would produce neuronic impacts because seeing our external "I"s being treated with respect would conflict with our intellectual "I"s which are accustomed to mistreatment.

Although empirical science has concluded that, with the exception of sensual pleasure, pleasure, like the mind, doesn't exist, we are motivated by the pleasure that we feel in the absence of neuronic impacts. Because we act to remove ourselves from the pain of neuronic impacts, we act to obtain nonsensual pleasure.

Learned opinion as encoded in empirical encyclicals disagrees with the idea that nonsensual pleasure is the absence of pain. However, we are all aware of the feeling of self-satisfaction that occasionally floods over us, just as we are all aware of the mind that rests behind our eyes between our ears and forms pictures of the world around us, so that talking about pleasure as the absence of pain should not produce too much pain.

While there may well be a biological basis for sexual pleasure, or sensuous pleasure, the pleasures of the flesh as it were, there is no empirical evidence that this feeling of self-satisfaction, or any other "feeling" of well-being, exists, so it is just a delusion, a passing fancy with no substance, anecdotal, as the empirically adept are wont to classify that which they disdain.

However, like the perception of pain, the perception of pleasure is a product of comparison. Pain either results from the mind's operation, the neuronic impacts that disrupt the subsystems, or directly, by contact with the circuits of the body that are designed to protect us, the sensors that cause us to reflexively move away from sources of pain.

Even the perception of the pain that results from cuts and burns require that the mind be operating, functioning, actually performing recall.

The horribly injured crash victim that doesn't remember anything until he wakes up in the hospital days later, and therefore doesn't remember having any pain, didn't have any pain because the shock of the accident stopped his recall function.

If the mind is not functioning, then nothing is being stored in recall.

If nothing is being stored in recall, nothing is being recalled, and if there is nothing being recalled, then there is no way to perceive the physical effect of the damage to the subsystems.

The perception of nonsensual pleasure requires a mind that is operating because the pleasure is produced by the absence of pain.

When our minds send electrical impulses into our muscles to move our bodies through physical reality, our bodies do not perceive the impact of those electrical impulses as pain. But after we have walked the mile and sit down to rest, the absence of those impulses sure feels good.

In like manner, as we go through our daily activities, we are constantly assaulted by neuronic impacts of one degree or another. The slob that lets the door slam shut in front of us, the elevator that doesn't come, the coworker that fails to say good morning, the boss that doesn't say good morning heartily enough, the fear that there is a piece of lettuce hanging off our chin, the assaults go on and on all day long.

When we get home, pull the door shut behind us and sit in our accustomed chair with whatever ablution we favor, we damn well feel relieved, relieved to be out of the battle, away from the front, safe and sound in familiar surroundings.

It is the absence of neuronic impacts that is making us feel good.

On the positive side, if during the day we have hit the bull's eyes, nailed the job, obtained the contract, brought home the bacon, thinking about the success will make us feel good because we are recalling our external "I"s as they should be, successful in their movement through physical reality, a picture which agrees with our intellectual "I"s which have to form a picture of our external "I"s moving successfully through physical reality.

Comprehension, understanding, the process of comparison, does produce physical pleasure, as does the absence of conflict, the cessation of pain.

What does or does not please us is determined by how our intellectual "I"s were shaped. The popular phrase, "Whatever turns you on." deals with the simple fact that our intellectual "I"s are a conglomeration of the millions of pictures we have formed and stored and which are available for recall, our unique experience, and how we as individuals have learned to use those experiences as we cope with the neuronic impacts that arise as we interact with others.

Doing whatever turns us on, however, is not a reliable way to operate a society! Attempting to maintain a positive intellectual "I", in fact, and carrying out acts to maintain that positive intellectual "I" is actually destructive to society because it leads to creating recall of ourselves in the positions of others.

When we deal with how the mind operates to produce the concepts of morality and law incorporated into societal institutions, the subjective pleasure and pain that result from the personal comparison compiled from experience must evolve into a picture of objective behavior that will guide our intellectual "I"s in determining how our external "I"s will behave, what acts our external "I"s will engage in in exchange for being a member of the society.

In short, with actions in physical reality being merely objective movements of animate matter in physical reality which seeks pleasure and attempts to avoid pain, how do some acts become immoral?

What's the difference between crushing a rock, chopping down a tree and shooting our neighbor?

I sidestepped this question in *The Model Mind*, refusing to explore the ramifications of either the formation of the intellectual "I" as a moral self, or the formation of the external "I" as a product of social conditioning. However, because I needed to have a moral reference point for the conflicts that cause us incessant pain, I fused the intellectual "I" as conditioned by both experience and morality into what I styled the idealistic "I". Because the purpose of *The Model Mind* was to demonstrate how the mind and the body function together, expanding the discussion to a third "I", a moral or societal "I" that embodied objective morality, risked losing the demonstration to needless complexity.

The fusion, however, conveniently sidestepped the question. It did not address the source of objective morality.

Worse, it directed attention away from the fact that the intellectual and external "I"s are evolutionary "I"s that come into existence as a result of the mind's operation in dealing with forthright reality and not as a result of the subsequent subjugation of the mind to the illusions that arise when it can recall realities when realities do not exist. Assuming away a moral intellectual "I" ignored the question of how the mind deals with nonapparent reality, how it produces recall for questions of motion and existence, or recall for realities that might, but don't, exist, the recall dealing with nonapparent reality and technology, and avoided the question of how we create the rules that control our interactions with one another so that we can live together without tearing each other apart.

It was only when I began to see society and the institutions society creates as a product of the mind's operation that I realized it was the need to make up recall to match nonapparent reality in order to avoid the pain that results when the mind cannot perform its evolved function of matching recall and reality that controls how we construct the morality that then governs our interactions with one another.

The difference between crushing a rock, chopping down a tree and shooting our neighbor is neuronic impacts!

Without neuronic impacts, there can be no morality.

And neuronic impacts only arise when we can view our external "I"s being thwarted in physical reality, mistreated.

When we see another attacked, we might experience a full range of emotions. We might be enraged because the attack is unprovoked, we might fear we will be attacked, we might be frustrated because we can't or won't help the person being attacked, we might feel guilt for being a part of the attack or we might feel remorse because we have to live in a world where such attacks are possible.

The emotions we experience result from picturing ourselves in the position of the person being mistreated.

When we see someone being attacked, we receive neuronic impacts because we can visualize our external "I"s being attacked and that conflicts with the positive picture of our intellectual "I"s we have to have in recall in order to move safely through physical reality.

How can visualizing an attack on our external "I"s cause neuronic impacts when there is no objective morality programmed into the inanimate matter that has been animated to produce our intellectual "I"s?

If we see a thug beating someone, we don't need much imagination to know that the person being beaten is hurting. Every blow, or imagining every blow, makes us wince mentally because we know that blows leave marks and marks hurt like hell.

When we see someone verbally abused, we are similarly discomfited because we know how we would feel if we were in the same situation.

Even if there were no morality, we would feel neuronic impacts from someone else's misfortune because we can imagine ourselves, our external "I"s, undergoing that same misfortune and that picture would conflict with the positive picture our intellectual "I"s have to have of our external "I"s acting in physical reality.

The neuronic impacts that imprint morality on the morally unwritten intellectual "I" come from the conflict produced by the inescapable comparison of the physical body that intellectual "I" is occupying existing without the physical blows or verbal abuse, existing without being under assault, existing in fact, intact, sitting unharmed, with the picture of the external "I" being forced into recall, the picture of the external "I" being viciously assaulted created by watching another person being viciously assaulted.

When our intellectual "I"s observe others in unfortunate circumstances, we will place our own external "I"s in those same circumstances and the resulting neuronic impacts will give rise to a sympathetic response which will tend to discourage us from doing things to others that we wouldn't want others doing to us.

And, while this is the golden rule embodied in Christian morality, every society, and even individual segments of a society, philosophers, for instance, come to the same conclusion dealing with the interrelationships of sentient animate matter, how we have to behave if we are to successfully live together.

Only it is not something that is concluded.

It is dictated by how our minds operate.

Any normal mind operates on the basis of recall and thus produces an intellectual "I" that observes a picture of the reality of which it is both the center, the observer, the self, and the actor, the external "I" in physical reality.

This is the basic structure of the mind, the natural result of the mechanism's operation, the function it evolved to carry out its purpose as a detector of physical reality. It is an inescapable process once the mind evolved to move the animate matter to which it is attached through physical reality.

It is the only way we have to move through physical reality.

Because our intellectual "I"s are a product of and in equilibrium with the animate matter that makes us up, and because we have to have a positive picture of ourselves acting in order for us to move through physical reality, our intellectual "I"s embody a picture of our external "I"s unbidden, unhindered, untouched as we move through physical reality.

However, because our intellectual "I"s are able to visualize things that do not exist in physical reality, we are able to combine observations of the misfortunes of others with the movement of our external "I"s in our imaginations, in our recall, creatively causing actions to occur to our external "I"s that have actually been visited on others, and, in doing so, producing a conflict between the picture that is inherent in our intellectual "I"s, the normal picture of our external "I"s not being subjected to any indignity and the picture of our external "I"s suffering the misfortunes of others.

The resulting conflict of recall with reality produces the neuronic impacts which makes our intellectual "I"s aware that we don't want the things we see visited on others and recall being visited on our external "I"s actually being visited on our external "I"s.

When it comes time for us to chose from our options, to select courses of action, our intellectual "I"s set up courses of action and test them against the neuronic impacts the pain each course of action might cause.

If we are walking down the street and we run into our neighbor's spouse and we form a picture of ourselves with our neighbor's spouse, we might allow serial recall to alter the picture from our neighbor's spouse in bed with us to our spouse in bed with our neighbor!

How we would want our neighbor to behave toward us might well determine how we behave toward our neighbor because we know that if our neighbor behaved toward us like we were planning to behave toward our neighbor, if we put our external "I" in the position of our neighbor, we know that we would be destroyed by the resulting pain.

In the day to day operations of society, when decisions are made about how people should act in society, when we sit down and pass laws that govern our behavior, the decisions we make are going to be made on the basis of whether we would want to prevent something from being done to our external "I"s.

The golden rule springs from the operation of the mind and it is a powerful determinant of the rules a society makes to control the behavior of its members.

The rules society makes to deal with the behavior of its members are based on how the rulemakers would like to be treated.

And we are all the rulemakers!

The resulting behavior is Golden Rule Behavior, and it embodies the morality of society.

If we violate Golden Rule Behavior, we can recall our external "I"s doing things which violate the morality that informs our intellectual "I"s and the resulting conflict produces neuronic impacts which we interpret as guilt.

Because we attempt to avoid the pain that guilt produces, we try to avoid the acts that would give rise to guilt.

Restraining ourselves from violating Golden Rule Behavior gives rise to moral behavior and because the moral behavior is based on an objective standard, how each member of society would like to be treated, it is objective morality.

However, we are not alone able to restrain ourselves from acting. Empathy may well produce an objective standard of morality, but without some way for that standard to produce neuronic impacts, it would not provide a bar to our actions.

Incorporating the standards into religious prohibitions is the primitive way for societies to dictate objective standards, but bare religious prohibitions are mere words which do not explain on an operational basis why we will voluntarily give up our freedom to act.

To understand why we are willing to restrain our behavior when we evolved to move through physical reality without restraint, we have to understand the difference between our god and our behavior.

3. THINGS FOR WHICH WE CAN HAVE NO RECALL

We create recall that we use to match the objects we encounter in reality. We create categories in our recall in which we place pictures of these objects so that when we see an object in reality we can recall a picture of the object for comparison. When our recall compares with reality, when we have recognition, we have understanding and we comprehend what we see in reality.

This comparison process provides us with satisfaction as the old light bulb goes off in our mind, the mental "Ah Ha!" which we feel as comprehension. Comprehension makes us feel good because when our recall doesn't compare with reality or when we have no recall to compare with reality, we feel neuronic impacts, discomfort.

When we match recall and reality, we are relieved of the expectation that we will be subject to the pain of not comprehending, the neuronic impacts that result when we can't match recall with reality.

In addition to simply existing in reality, objects in reality also do things in reality.

They move!

Because we do not want to experience discomfort when we see objects doing something in physical reality, and because we automatically classify objects in reality to avoid the discomfort that occurs when we don't have recall for what we see, we do the same thing we do with objects in reality when we see something happening, we create recall that will allow us to have the same feeling of comprehension we have when we see something that just exists.

We can't see what is causing what we see, so we make up words, gravity, angular momentum, moving charges, labels and laws that, because they cause us to believe we have comprehended what we see, make up the occult mixture of ignorance and superstition that is empirical science.

The distinction between objects and what objects do is not the same as the dichotomy between matter and nothing because, while we can never know where matter comes from, if we are careful to limit ourselves to current mechanical explanations for the nature of the forces that cause matter to move as opposed to simulating understanding by encasing the nature of force in the ignorance of words and then contenting ourselves with merely describing the result of the force, the movement, we can produce a consistent picture of how the physical reality which includes ourselves operates.

One of the primary things that objects do in reality, and which produces all of the movement in reality, is come apart in the process of combustion, burning, active reduction, whatever it happens to be styled. The term combustion has been theoretically limited in the twentieth century, the mindless century, a century in which rational inquiry into the nature of physical reality has been abandoned in favor of quasi-religious belief systems that merely use words, incantations, to explain effects.

Combustion refers to the chemical combination of matter with oxygen, a limitation that underscores our inability to distinguish between objects in reality and our occult interpretations about the nature and movement of those objects in reality. Our occult interpretations, which we embody in words, limit our inquiries into physical reality — with "combustion", what causes the production of light — but we make up occult interpretations and give them names which allow us to accept them as fact, forever blinding ourselves to the light of reality.

For the lack of a better term, I use combustion to describe what occurs when light and other frequencies are produced.

Matter combusts!

When matter combusts, it comes apart, and if matter comes apart, then it certainly had to come together in a process of matter formation, a concept that doesn't exist in empirical science *which measures matter* to be created in the center of stars.

If we take the electron to be what we measure it to be, a particle that has a charge that attracts other electrons, as opposed to a particle that repels other electrons, and if, in addition, we take the electron to be a particle that also moves at the speed of light when it isn't restrained from moving by a conductor, the tissue of a nerve or some other substance, a fact demonstrated by its ability to regain its speed after it has been slowed down, then it is fairly simple to see electrons forming into units which form into nuclei of atoms which attract orbiting electrons and combine into matter.

It is also apparent that this matter, once formed, will come apart into its constituent electrons when it is immersed in flows of moving electrons, the light that is produced by combustion.

We see it happen every time we throw a log on the fire!

When electrons make up matter, the charge that is a property of the electron holds the matter together. When electrons are held together into matter, their charge is restraining what would otherwise be their normal motion, which is motion at the speed of light.

When matter, made up of electrons whose charges have overcome their motion, is immersed in a strong enough field, the charge of the field, itself made up of electrons, becomes a substitute for the charge holding the electrons together into matter, and with the charges holding the matter together replaced, the electrons making up the matter regain their motion, organizing themselves into frequencies which include light and depart the area at the speed of light.

The matter formation portion of the equation occurs when there is no combustion, no emission field. With no emission field to occupy the charges of the electrons, the charges of the electrons can attract one another and the electrons can form into units that form into nuclei which attract orbiting electrons and combine into matter.

Energy therefore is simply the basic particle of matter, electrons, held together by their charges into matter, regaining their motion.

Matter, however, does more than come apart in combustion and form back together into physical matter.

Physical matter moves!

Matter drops to the surface of the Earth in a specific manner, accelerating inversely with the square of the distance over which it moves. Emissions produced by combustion mirrors this measurement, producing expanding frequencies such as light which diminish inversely with the square of the distance over which they expand.

Because matter mathematically falls in expanding emission fields at the same rate those emission fields expand, it is not hard to draw the mathematical connection that expanding emission fields induce movement back toward the source of the emitted frequencies.

Knowing that emission fields are composed of electrical flows, knowing that electrical flows produce inductances, flows of electrons that move at right angles to the electrical flows, and knowing that frequencies such as light, although convertible to electricity, have no measurable charge, we can visualize the charges of the electrons that make up emission fields balanced by the charges of their associated inductances resulting in the lack of a measurable charge in light.

The emissions from two combusting bodies in space induce rotation in each other as a result of the inductances associated with the flows each emits and the dominate emitter, the hottest of the two, the one producing the strongest emission field, as a result of the reverse bias of the expanding emission field that results from the rotation of the emitter, induces the other emitters to orbit it, producing the solar system we have with moons orbiting planets and planets orbiting the sun, and the large structure star systems called galaxies, where the stars all orbit a mathematical point established by the sum total of the stars' emission fields which are being emitted and trailing back behind their direction of rotation, the stars that make up the structure slowly falling in their direction of rotation.

All of these things that are happening to matter are the natural result of the two properties of the electron, attraction and motion, which produce a universe in which matter comes into existence in areas of nothingness where there is no field. Starlight pours into pockets of space as the starlight expands out of existence and the charges of the electrons that make up the starlight reorganize themselves into matter which eventually encounters fields of starlight, ignites and forms into the galaxies and solar systems which we see burning brightly in nothingness, emitting the electrons that make them up in frequencies which expand out into space, producing motion in other matter as they do so until they expand out of existence in other pockets of space and reform into matter.

The expanding emission fields attract nonemitting matter into the source of the emissions, causing all matter to emit and recycle itself back into its constituent electrons.

This is the cycle of matter in the universe and the movement of matter in nothingness.

But this is an interpretation of how matter acts in the universe. We can carry the interpretation forward to explain life if we understand that life, animate matter, is the organization of atoms and molecules of atoms, the structures electrons and atoms produce, around electrical flows in the environment.

Because emission fields produce rotation and orbiting, one emitter becomes dominate, producing a solar system. As all matter cools off at a similar rate, the less dominate emitters in the solar system cool faster than the more dominate emitters. Thus, a small sphere of matter such as the Earth cools off while the dominant emitter, the sun, is still visibly emitting. As the Earth cools, it forms a crust which is made up of different elements that have broken down in the strong field of the combusting surface as it congealed.

These different elements each have an electrical potential that we can measure as different from each of the other elements.

The cooling Earth is rotating in front of the dominant emitter, the sun, and as it does so it is passing from night to day and back again to night. This constant movement constantly changes the temperature of the elements on the Earth's surface.

A measurable result of temperature change in elements is a change in the element's potential difference.

Thus, as the cooling Earth rotated in front of the sun, the elements on its surface continually underwent changes in electrical potential with respect to one another, and electrical flows, which we measure moving between differences in potential, were constantly moving back and forth across the surface of the planet as it congealed out of a molten mass into a diversity of elements.

As the light elements condensed into an atmosphere, they produced atoms and molecules of atoms that were capable of forming around those electrical flows, and animate matter, life, began to cover the surface of the cooling Earth.

Once life formed, the only thing that prevented it from forming complexity was the heat. As the Earth cooled, however, animate matter evolved the complexity that allowed it to first become ambulatory, move around in the environment and thus become independent of local conditions, and then become sentient, learn how to manipulate the environment to its own benefit, thereby further extending its range of survivability in the environment.

Life forms on Earth all the time as conditions permit, but it only evolved once because life develops the complexity necessary to deal with a changing environment as that environment changes, as a planet on which it develops cools.

And, if we realize that the mind is merely the detector that evolved to move animate matter through the environment, we can, without too much mental effort, figure out how it can form pictures of that environment that are common to all detectors in the environment so that when we see a tree we not only recall a tree, we all recall the same tree.

Frequencies produced by combustion expand over the surface of an expanding sphere which diminishes inversely with the distance over which the sphere expands. Not only do these frequencies, emissions, diminish, they do so uniformly. It is this fact of uniform expansion that gives the clue to the nature of the mechanism that causes matter caught in expanding emission fields to move back toward the source of the emissions. But it is the uniform expansion itself that allows us to form relatively uniform pictures of external reality, the pictures varying from person to person only because each person comprehends what he or she sees with their unique recall, the particular memory units that make up each individual's stored experience.

Because emissions from combusting matter diminish uniformly, the emissions contain information. We can't take the emissions at one point and determine the rate at which the source that is producing them is combusting, but we can take the emissions at one point in an expanding sphere of emissions and compare them with the strength of the emissions at another point in the expanding sphere of emissions because all of the emissions are diminishing with the square of their distance from the source, and the source is the same. Because the emissions are electrons and therefore have a charge, having a detector that evolved to detect the charge, rather than just the temperature, allows us to pinpoint our relative position at any point in an emission field.

But we did not evolve floating in an emission field. We evolved in an environment on the surface of the Earth made up of the sharp edges of physical reality. When light from the sun is bouncing off those hard edges, it is reexpanding over the surface of new expanding spheres. The eye, at any position in the environment, receives these flows, all expanding over the surfaces of different expanding spheres, and measures exactly how strong one emission flow is in comparison with another emission flow.

Because the strength of the flow provides information about distance, the eye collects information about the relative distances to all of the hard edges in physical reality by collecting the diminishing flows of light from those hard edges as sunlight bounces off of them.

This is the information that is transported by the optic nerve to the mind which then uses it to create a representation, form a picture of the external reality in which the eye is located.

Again, all of this is interpretation, although because we are using mechanical explanations of current forces instead of ignoring force and merely describing effects with words, the resulting picture of physical reality is moving away from the occult and coming closer to actually explaining what is occurring when matter moves in reality.

How do we know our interpretations about what happens in physical reality are correct?

Facts in physical reality do not provide meaning. We don't understand facts. A rock is a rock and there isn't much else to know about it unless we want to start categorizing rocks, and then we are only organizing facts, not understanding anything.

The only way that we can understand something is by comparing the facts we see in physical reality with the recall we have about those facts.

The recall is not reality, and the recall can never be reality. We can never say any particular interpretation about physical reality is correct because interpretations about physical reality are merely recall. Empirical science claims its interpretations about physical reality, meaningless statements such as objects fall because gravity is a property of matter, planets rotate — and therefore the sun comes up — because angular momentum is conserved in closed systems, planets orbit because they condensed out of a swirling mass of gas, electricity is a moving charge, light a wave and magnetism the result of molecular magnets, to be fact because of a scientific method that claims that recall that predicts facts can prove the recall.

Because recall about objects in reality, recall that is an interpretation of how objects in reality move, how they formed, how they come apart, can never be more than that, recall, a made-up interpretation that is used to explain the facts in reality, that recall is never very far away from the recall that deals with things for which we can never have any recall because there is no reality the recall can interpret, the question of where matter came from in the first place.

We have to be extremely careful not to mix up the things for which we can produce a mechanical explanation, the source of force and the nature of motion, with those things we have to take on the basis of revelation, matters related to the mere existence of physical matter for which we produce religion. Empirical science's explanations for physical reality, gravity, light waves, moving charges, angular momentum and the like are never more than one step away from religion because they don't seek to explain anything, they are just a process of putting words in recall so that when we see something, we can recall the words and we won't feel the pain neuronic impacts produce when we see something for which we have no recall.

Much of the consensus belief of empirical science is driven by the need to avoid the pain of not knowing, to shield the practitioners of empirical science and the populace they serve from the shock of having no recall for the obvious things in reality, falling objects and sunrises, not to mention the fear of the embarrassment that would result from the discovery that, while claiming to know everything, it knows nothing.

The nonanswers of empirical science result from the same effort to avoid pain, to shield the body against neuronic impacts, that produces religions, concepts of god, although listening to anthropologists would lead us to think otherwise.

We have all heard the narrative. Primitive men, barely distinguishable from their ape parents, venture out from the safety of the forest to the danger of the lowlands where a bolt of lightening streaks down from the sky. Startled, awe struck, frightened half to death, the scraggly band goes scurrying back into the forest where, stopping in front of the first cave they come upon, they build a little mound of rocks to appease the source of the fright, the sky from whence the lightening came.

Getting their courage back up, the little band makes another attempt at invading the fruited plains, this time making it all the way to a juicy mastodon where its members immediately invent tools that can be used to carve up dinner, and, in the process, begin the ascent to civilization, an ascent marred only by that pesky little altar in front of the cave which the primitives now insist on recognizing for their good fortune by offering up a hairy mastodon leg in supplication, giving rise to religion.

The facts of history are as forever out of our reach as are the interpretations for what makes matter move and therefore are not facts, but rather interpretations. Making up historical scenarios to explain things like religion is rather presumptuous when religion is the natural glue of all societies, stickier even than civil government and judicial systems, the two being inseparable from religion in early societies.

Religion and the concept of a god is produced by the operation of the mind!

Religious questions, where did we come from?, where did the world come from?, why are we here?, and where do we go when we die?, are not the questions of morality, why do we do things that make us feel bad?, why do we hurt other people?, and will we pay for hurting ourselves and others when we get to where we go when we die? although both are implicit in the mind's operation.

Religious questions are obvious realities dealing with the existence of physical matter, the universe and ourselves, for which we can have no recall!

Not only are religious questions questions for which we can have no recall, they are questions for which we can have no interpretation because interpretation presupposes that we have something happening that can be interpreted.

Simple existence is not something that is happening.

Simple existence is simply something, like matter in nothingness.

It can have no explanation.

If we go back to the dichotomies between objects and motion, matter and nothing, motion can lead to interpretations of the physical reality dealing with the source of the force producing the motion because we are dealing with something that is actually happening while existence is the fact of matter, nothing more.

There is nothing more that can be explained.

We exist, matter exists, we are matter and that's it.

We can never know where the matter came from, how the individual particle that makes up our universe and ourselves came into existence.

But the very existence of matter is a fact. If we don't have something in recall to compare with the various aspects of reality raised by simple existence, then we will receive neuronic impacts every time we pause and contemplate our existence and the existence of the universe.

We are not driven to construct religious systems because of lightening sending its electric bolt into the ground, crashing into our consciousness as it barely misses our puny bodies, we are driven to construct religious systems because the failure to do so sends neuronic impacts, electrical discharges directly into the subsystems that make up our bodies, causing us indescribable pain with no apparent source.

We have to construct a god to protect ourselves from our recall having nothing to match the fact of our existence!

Once our minds form, and once we becomes sentient and obtain the ability to form pictures of reality where reality does not exist, then we begin to recognize our own existence and we begin to see our bodies as a part of the pictures of reality that we form with our minds.

Once we see ourselves in the pictures we form of reality, we begin to develop a picture of our self, the intellectual "I" that is looking out at that picture of ourselves, at our external "I".

As soon as we become aware of ourselves aware of ourselves, we want to know where we came from. We move past the primitive instinct, which might inform us that we have a third eye in our forehead that is looking out upon ourselves acting, or that we have an invisible presence standing somewhere behind us looking over our shoulder as we act, and develop a concept of a god that created us.

Once we have a god that created us, then we are in the position of an empirical scientist with his gravity, molecular magnets or swirling masses of gas, we have a word that we can bring into recall when we ask the question, "Where did we come from?", a word that provides an answer, "God created us!", and therefore simulate comprehension, understanding, by eliminating the pain not knowing produces.

Of course, knowing what makes objects drop, how a magnet works, or why planets orbit might be exceedingly useful information if we wanted to extend our range of survivability in physical reality, and failing to address these questions in order to obtain actual answers would be a crime of considerable proportion, if crime is defined as doing something against the interests of our continued existence.

However, with respect to the question basic to religion, the question of simple existence for which there can be no recall, any answer that stops the pain is appropriate.

This gives us a general proposition that questions of belief in a superior creator are questions of personal preference, private affairs, a proposition that is confirmed by the existence of the many religious systems at the basis of the various societies on Earth and even the existence of many different religious systems within a specific society.

The production of religious systems as a result of self-awareness, however, has nothing to do with the production of morality!

Different religious systems produce different moral systems, and different moral systems will produce massive neuronic impacts when mixed. Our intellectual "I"s, versed in one moral system will come into conflict with our external "I"s when we see our moral system violated by our neighbor who is versed in another moral system. Seeing others act in reality causes us to attempt to form pictures of our external "I"s engaging in those same acts, and when reality forces us to form pictures of our external "I"s engaged in acts that violate our moral concepts, the resulting neuronic impacts produce rage which is directed at the person causing the thoughts, the person performing the repugnant acts, our neighbor.

Moral systems do not evolve to explain our existence, they evolve to produce a standard of conduct that will allow us to come together into societies.

The existence of our god is basic to our self-awareness. We have to create a god of some sort, even if it is a denial of a god, which we can put into our recall to explain existence because we do not have in recall, nor can we have in recall, anything based on physical reality that will explain our simple existence.

Morality, on the other hand, comes into existence to control our behavior when we interact with others.

However, in nascent societies, religion is inseparable from morality. Primitive societies also subsume governmental authority, judicial authority and questions of science, areas of existence for which there actually can be knowledge of reality.

If we define science as knowledge rather than as a system of laws governing the operation of nature, which is merely another way of saying God, we can start to separate knowledge about the operations of physical reality from the ignorance and superstition that is inherent in primitive religious systems.

When we first ask where we came from and why we are here, when we first question existence, all matter is existence, and the question extends its umbrella to all existence, and thus to all questions about all matter, about rocks and trees and other facts in reality, and about moving rocks and burning trees, about things that are happening in reality.

We can not readily separate questions that belong in the realm of religion from questions that belong in the realm of science, objective knowledge, because when we make up pictures about reality that are not contradicted in reality, and place those pictures in recall, we mistake what we have made up for reality.

As a primitive society becomes aware of itself, it has to sort out which areas of existence, objects, force, motion and existence belong in the realm of belief, produce questions for which made-up answers will have to suffice and which areas of reality will produce questions about physical reality that will generate pictures of physical possibilities that will allow the society to extend itself into the future.

A society that believes that all of reality is in the provenance of its gods, that the answers to all questions are a matter of faith and belief, will live out its existence in place, never venturing out to discover physical reality.

A less primitive society might be able to visualize the actual objects that make up physical reality as something that is not in the provenance of the gods and thus something that might be manipulated to the benefit of society. Unless religion wanted a particular object for an icon, an amulet, as something imbued with sacred spirit, then objects could simply be objects in reality, matter that could be separated by its properties and characteristics, and classified by measuring, naming and categorizing.

We always fear challenging our gods, even if we don't believe in them, because our gods represent the unknown, that portion of reality for which we can have no recall. A society that freed objects from the provenance of its gods would still be controlled by ignorance and superstition if it left questions of force and motion up to its gods.

A society that has not confronted the basic questions of physical reality, the nature of force, its source and how it causes motion, could well manipulate objects in physical reality to its benefit, but any manipulation would be merely the product of chance trial and error. Without a direct analysis of force and the nature of motion, such a society could manufacture its explanations for the technology it created like it manufactured its explanations for its gods, anything would be acceptable so long as it wasn't directly contradicted by physical reality.

Only primitive superstitious societies would mix up recall dealing with the source of force and the nature of motion with the recall dealing with the source of existence. Only an ignorant and superstitious society would make the mistake of concluding that force and motion were created when matter was created by the creator of the matter and placed in that matter as a property of the matter.

Only a primitive and superstitious society could delude itself into believing that objects move in straight lines unless a force acts to change the straight-line motion because motion is a part of the matter and that the force that alters straight-line motion, the force that causes objects to drop, is a property of matter.

The force that causes motion exists and requires recall that explains in a mechanical way how that motion comes about. Without a mechanical explanation for motion, the force that causes motion remains a part of the religious explanations that are made up to explain the existence of matter, where we come from, where the universe came from, where we go when we cease to exist, things for which we can have no recall and thus for which all recall is acceptable.

We don't receive neuronic impacts when we classify a rock, and we don't receive neuronic impacts when we recall a god as the answer for our own existence, but we do receive neuronic impacts when we see things move without apparent force.

If we use religious answers to explain physical facts, to explain questions of force and energy, questions of motion, God created the universe and all the movement in it, then we will not be answering the questions raised by physical existence and we will not be able to extend our range of survivability in physical reality.

On the other hand, if we are satisfied with using words, classifying physical facts that require explanation, if we use words to explain questions of energy, and force and motion, swirling masses of gas create straight-line motion which is altered by the mass of the gas, then we are going to be doubly ignorant, because thinking we have avoided explaining physical reality with religious explanations, we are going to believe that the words provide us with the explanation, and we are going to do so because the answer does not provide us with neuronic impacts, with pain.

We are not driven to find the answers to the real questions of physical reality, questions of force and motion, because we think we already know the answers!

Like force and motion, the source of our morality also presents an area in which we have to discern between what is a necessary component of existence and what is a product of the explainable interaction of matter, in our case, of animate matter.

Inanimate objects do not raise questions of morality. It is only when atoms and molecules of atoms organize themselves around electrical flows that matter evolves detectors which allow movement within the environment that questions of morality arise.

Because morality deals with standards of behavior, how we should or should not act, standards whose source is not apparent, primitive societies confuse questions dealing with its source, as they do with questions of force and motion, with the source of existence, with the gods and place the authority for the restraint on actions morality dictates with those things for which there can be no recall.

However, if moral authority, the restraint on our actions, is viewed as a product of the mind, as the strategy the mind evolves when the organisms to which it is attached are driven together into a society, then a mechanical explanation of the source and operation of that authority becomes something for which we can have recall.

4. THE UBIQUITOUS "I"

Our minds generate external "I"s so that we can form a picture of ourselves in recall moving through physical reality and thus actually move through physical reality. Without a picture of ourselves in relation to the reality in which we exist, we would not be able to move about in that reality.

Our intellectual "I"s are a simple by-product of the mind's operation. All of the pictures that our minds form of physical reality contain a viewpoint centered around the mind forming the pictures.

Awareness of that viewpoint does not occur until the mind becomes sentient.

Sentience occurs when we become desensitized to the neuronic impacts that occur when we attempt to form a picture of reality that does not exist in reality. When our minds reach the point that we can recall a reality that is not present, when our minds can hold a picture that has no agreement in reality against the pain of the neuronic impacts from the conflict the recall produces, then the awareness of ourselves aware of ourselves, our awareness of our intellectual "I"s, begins to emerge.

Without physical reality present, we first recall a picture of ourselves, our external "I"s in a physical reality, that does not presently exist in physical reality, and then we recall a picture of our self, our viewpoint, an awareness that there is an "I", something that is viewing our external "I"s existing in physical reality.

Our eyes are our primary sensory organ. They are located where they can best transmit sensory input dealing with the position of our external "I"s as they move through physical reality. Because the mind uses the eyes as its primary input, our minds are located close to our eyes. Because the wet works of the brain is where the mind stores recall, our minds are chemically embedded in our brains, undetectable structures made up of electrons held into a stable web of equilibrium. As awareness occurs in our minds, our concept of self is located behind the eyes and between the ears.

But once an awareness of self occurs, once we become aware of our intellectual "I"s, then we have a perpetual puzzle about where that self, that invisible, undetectable viewpoint comes from.

Being able to actually see portions of our physical bodies in physical reality does not increase our ability to move through physical reality because we are always aware of where the structures that move our bodies, our arms and our legs, are. We need a picture of physical reality in recall in order to place our bodies in appropriate places with respect to that physical reality.

As long as we are occupied locating our bodies with respect to physical reality, as long as we are moving in physical reality, our minds and bodies are doing what they evolved to do. We eat food which is broken down into energy, the electricity that operates our bodies and our minds. As our eyes feed pictures of reality to our minds, our minds form pictures of our bodies in our recall. If we are driven by hunger to get more energy, then our minds produce recall of a reality that does not exist, we picture ourselves in recall slicing open the belly of the fleeting gazelle, and we move through physical reality in an attempt to turn recall into reality, to get the food we need to fill our stomachs.

Each picture we form in our recall of our body moving through physical reality is formed slightly ahead of our body's realization of the picture in actual reality. At any one time, our minds have many minor conflicts dealing with the location of our body parts with respect to physical reality. While massive conflicts might stop us in our tracks, the minor conflicts carry out the evolved purpose of our minds to move our bodies through physical reality.

Each minor conflict, for instance our hand at our side needing to scratch our nose, will stop the operation of our mind with respect to that conflict, sending the resulting electrical signals to the appropriate muscles in our body. If our hand is by our side in reality, but by our nose in recall, the conflict dealing with one element of the overall picture of reality our mind is constructing, our hand, will cause that portion of our mind to stop operating, sending the electrical signals that are no longer operating that part of our mind to the part of our body that that portion of our mind is keeping track of, our hand. Our hand, getting a jolt of electricity, has to move to dissipate it, and serial recall and successive jolts cause our hand to move to our nose.

These directed neuronic flows make the picture of reality in recall a reality that exists in reality.

This is how our minds move the matter that makes us up, our bodies, through physical reality.

If we are somehow prevented from moving our hand, creating a reality that doesn't exist in recall, then our overall picture of physical reality will be narrowed to include only our hand, and, because we can't move our hand, the directed neuronic flows become massive neuronic impacts as the entire focus of our mind now becomes centered on the picture of our blocked hand.

Not being able to scratch an itch results in incessant neuronic impacts which drive us insane, a common torture in the Gulag where recalcitrant prisoners were staked out to endure the hoards of hungry Arctic mosquitoes.

When we are able to move freely through physical reality, our minds are performing their evolved function and we have little awareness of its operation.

However, when we are not moving through physical reality, we are still recalling. Our minds cease to function in furtherance of their evolved purpose but they are still functioning!

In simple animate matter with a "mind" that merely senses temperature, the absence of temperature means the mind is not operating, is not detecting. When we sleep, a random recall function occurs as the electrons that make up the mind, disbalanced from continual use in forming pictures of physical reality, move back into their positions of stable equilibrium producing in the process the images we recall as dreams, but when the random recall function is not working, the mind is not working, and it is simply not detecting.

When we evolve to the point that we don't have to constantly be obtaining food or sleeping, when we can give our minds a rest from the constant conflicts we encounter as we move through physical reality in our drive to obtain food, then we can take the time to look around at the sunset and falling objects in physical reality and become poets or inventors.

When our minds aren't driven to do what they evolved to do, move us safely through physical reality, then we become very much aware of our intellectual "I"s, our invisible point of view, our "self", and we become aware of our intellectual "I"s recalling pictures of our external "I"s having done things in external physical reality.

We might have a picture of our external "I" spearing a fish. The serial recall that occurs as our focus shifts on individual elements of the pictures we form in our recall producing in the process current levels that recall related elements stored at similar current levels might carry our recall process through the cooking and eating of the fish. Serial recall creates moving pictures of reality as specific elements of a particular picture are called into focus. We form pictures of the fish, the fish in the pan, the pan on the fire, the fire cooking the fish, the fish cooked, the cooked fish in our mouth. This is all perfunctory serial recall going on without producing neuronic impacts that would cause us to stop moving positively through physical reality.

But what if our intellectual "I" allows our external "I" to go out and spear a fish, and we lose our balance, fall head first into the water, and then surface to the laughter of our companions who actually exist in physical reality?

Our external "I" which moments before was a creature of our recall, all of a sudden becomes a physical reality, something that actually exists in physical reality!

Our flub has become an act, something that has actually happened in physical reality. While the act itself no longer exists in physical reality, the water has moved on, we are drying off, we will later catch our dinner, cook and eat it, the flub will live on in the minds of everyone who has seen it because it is recallable by all. If our companions are good at building pictures with words, they can create recall of our flub in people who didn't even see it and the story of our flub will spread far and wide.

It is not pleasant recall because it involves a picture of our external "I" in reality disagreeing with the positive picture of our external "I" we need to have in recall in order to move through physical reality. The conflict produces neuronic impacts we recognize as ridicule. When others bring up our flub, the neuronic impacts are viewed as ridicule, and when the story travels far and wide, we are constantly confronted by neuronic impacts and consider ourself, the reality of our external "I" now transferred to and a part of our intellectual "I", a figure of ridicule.

As a result, the recall of us slipping is a collective recall, something that is more real than reality itself because we can see our external "I" in our recall falling over and over and over again and we know that everyone else can do the same.

Because we have to maintain a positive picture of our external "I" in order to move safely through physical reality, the majority of the pictures we have of our external "I" in recall are pictures of our external "I" acting successfully in physical reality, and the viewpoint of our intellectual "I" is one of positive accomplishment.

Thus, lying abed that night trying to go to sleep, the recall of ourselves ending up ass-end-over-tea-kettle in three feet of swiftly flowing water conflicts with the picture we have of ourselves in our intellectual "I" and we receive neuronic impacts every time we recall the fall. If we could see the humor in it, we might be able to shrug it off, say "I don't care," which is our intellectual "I"s abdicating a picture of self that could conflict with anything.

Our companions had certainly seen the humor in it!

Humor is the response to the abrupt substitution of an unexpected picture for the picture that is in recall. As all of our companions had gone about their fishing tasks, they had expected not only to work efficiently themselves, but they had expected to see everyone else work efficiently. Suddenly presented with the untoward reality of one of their number flailing about in the water like the fish they were trying to spear, they were suddenly presented with a picture of reality that was not in recall and their minds stopped operating. However, because the picture did not affect their intellectual "I"s and did not require them to do anything, did not require them to take action in reality, they were able to work the unexpected neuronic impacts off in a good thigh slapping laugh, the muscles closest to the mind, those around the eyes and the mouth, responding the most.

If we don't take kindly to being laughed at, if experience has taught us to dwell on our neuronic impacts, especially in the darkness of our recall, then lying abed recalling the flub over and over, imagining ourselves the butt of incessant ridicule, could produce a great deal of anger, the response to the pain of neuronic impacts, which would have to find an outlet in physical activity that would dissipate the electrons that make up the unwanted neuronic impacts.

If we didn't want to get up and do something that would dissipate the electrons, for instance, run around the campfire, we might try to stop the neuronic impacts by attempting to recall things that were more agreeable. We can only have one picture in recall at any one time so that thinking of something other than our flub would eliminate recall of the flub and thus eliminate our neuronic impacts.

Creating serial recall that shows our external "I" reaching down, picking up a rock and bashing in the head of the laughing face next to us would be more pleasant recall and would replace the picture of our flubbing external "I", eliminating the conflict with our positive intellectual "I" and thus the neuronic impacts associated with our flub.

Bashing in a laughing head would stop the laughter and also produce agreement with our intellectual "I" which doesn't like being laughed at. The agreement feels good because it stops our neuronic impacts.

The steps to relief are simple.

Recall of the flub forces us to serially recall our tormentor laughing at us and we feel the pain of neuronic impacts.

We substitute a picture of the laughing head with a bashed in head.

We have replaced a picture causing us pain with a picture that provides us with relief from pain and even provides us with a good feeling, perhaps pleasure.

The problem with seeking pleasure in creating recall of imagined revenge, however, is that our actions tend to follow the pictures of reality we form in our recall.

If the offense we are carrying around in our recall is great enough, and the resulting neuronic impacts torment us long enough, replaying the same recall that fends off the neuronic impacts, recalling over and over our tormentor's head bashed in, will increase the likelihood that we will take the action in reality we are continually creating in our recall. If a specific member of the group of our laughing companions also happens to be someone who has long tormented us, and laughing at the flub turns out to be the last straw, then all of our attempts to assuage the pain of our neuronic impacts by replacing a negative picture in our recall with a positive picture might well center on this one person.

The cycle then becomes, recall of the flub, recall of the laughing face of our tormentor, neuronic impacts, recall of our tormentor's laughing head bashed in, relief from the pain of the neuronic impacts, recall of the flub, recall of the laughing face of our tormentor, return of the neuronic impacts, and so on, over and over and over until the light of day delivers us to reality.

Every time we recall the flub, we have serial recall of our external "I" bashing in the brains of our imaginary tormentor.

Thus, the next day, when we gather to go fishing, and our tormentor makes a casual joke about checking our pockets for frogs, we recall the flub which serially leads to the pictures of imagined revenge and we pick up a rock and bash his head in.

Now we have left real tracks in physical reality!

We have a dead body and we have the recall of everybody that witnessed what appeared to be an unprovoked assault. No one is aware that we spent the night sitting up reliving the flub and getting relief by forming recall of what is now a reality, our brained companion lying in a pool of blood.

The first thing all of our companions are going to see when they look at their dead companion lying in a pool of blood with his head bashed in is their own external "I" lying on the ground in a pool of blood with his own head bashed in and each is going to receive the pain of neuronic impacts as a result. The extent of the neuronic impacts might vary from one to the other depending on what each thought of the dead man, what their relationship was, and some might be so blasé that they have to pretend concern, but collectively, it is not a good situation for the group when one member attacks another, and especially not when there is little or no provocation for the attack.

Each member of the group sees himself as the victim!

Nothing in this scenario deals with abstruse questions of human nature, fight or flight, territoriality, genetic predisposition or environmental conditioning. We are simply dealing with the result of a mind that evolved to move us through physical reality and which, to do so, evolved a recall system that allows us to form a picture of the physical reality through which we have to move, directing electrical flows into our bodies when the pictures of physical reality do not agree with the pictures we are forming in our recall, and which also produces a viewpoint, our intellectual "I"s that have a positive picture of our external "I"s which can conflict with the pictures of our external "I"s in physical reality resulting in the same electrical flows entering our bodies as neuronic impacts.

Electrical flows not only move the muscles that move us through physical reality, they cause us to act in physical reality in certain ways. Because neuronic impacts cause us pain, and because we reflexively seek to put ourselves in a position that eliminates pain, we are driven to act by the neuronic impacts produced when we have recall of our external "I"s that disagree with the positive picture of our external "I"s we have to maintain in order to move through physical reality.

Our minds evolved to move us through physical reality by creating a picture of ourselves in physical reality that has yet to occur in physical reality in order that we may extend our range of survivability in physical reality. The mind as a detector is a successful mechanism that allows us, as animate matter, to move through physical reality without bumping into trees or falling off of cliffs.

The by-product of this successful mechanism, awareness, is not a part of the evolved purpose of the mind.

The by-product of awareness, the creation of an intellectual "I" that can then turn around and produce neuronic impacts by forming pictures of our external "I"s that disagree with the positive picture of our external "I"s in our intellectual "I"s presents an entirely new set of problems.

Self-awareness allows us to produce conflicts that do not exist in reality, conflicts that, as a result of the evolved purpose of the mind, cause us neuronic impacts, real pain.

We can manufacture realities that don't exist in physical reality but which, because they cause us pain, drive us to act in reality.

We end up acting in reality, laying down tracks in physical reality, based on the recall of a reality that doesn't exist in physical reality!

The painless directed flows that evolved to move us through physical reality become incessant pain when they are created by conflicts that do not exist in reality, that do not arise as part of the process involved in moving us through physical reality.

The ability to create a recall that doesn't exist in reality, and thus produce imagined pictures of reality that create conflicts that lead to neuronic impacts and pain is a potential defect in the operation of the mechanism of the mind that could well result in our elimination, like a peacock feather evolved to promote procreation turning out to activate the peacock's own salivary glands.

However, an additional by-product of the mechanism that evolved to move us through physical reality, the ability of the mind to form pictures of a reality that does not exist in reality is the ability to actually create a physical reality that did not exist in reality before we created it in our recall. The resulting conflict of our recall with reality drives us to build spires in the sky and create technology that extends our range of survivability by making us independent of the environment in which we evolved.

We are literally caught between the hell of self-generated pain, suffering from the imagined slights of those around us, and the heaven of producing a technology that will carry us beyond our physical wants to inhabit the spires we create in the sky.

If we chose, through superstition and ignorance, to redress pain, real or imagined, we will spend our time lashing out at our neighbors, using our ability to create technology to make more effective rocks to bust heads rather than to find better ways to pile them into spires.

The use of our ability to create reality in our recall where reality does not exist to produce imagined slights that drive us to destructive behavior is the defect identified in *The Model Mind*, the defect that drives us to act in response to pain in ways that are not appropriate to our continued survival. In *Human Nature*, we are describing how this defect, inimical to the formation of a society necessary to direct the ability to produce an accurate technology that allows us to extend our range of survivability in physical reality, is mediated by the interactions that produce the society, the interactions that provide the standard of conduct that is the glue that holds society together.

We are animate matter driven to avoid pain, so the question is whether the pain of imagined slights will drive us to extinction before we can use the pain of recalling an unrealized reality as a driving force to extend our range of survivability, not just on this planet, but in the universe.

Everything that we do in physical reality we do as a result of forming a picture of our external "I"s doing those things in physical reality. And we form a picture of ourselves doing things in physical reality because we are driven to form those pictures. We are driven to form pictures by neuronic impacts and the only way neuronic impacts are produced is by conflicts of reality with recall, or conflicts of recall with reality.

Society attempts to mediate the responses that drive us to seek revenge in order to provide us with an opportunity to direct our efforts at extending our range of survivability in physical reality.

As we stand facing our companions over the dead body of our recently departed tormentor, our mind starts to return to normal, operating by having recall match reality instead of the made-up reality that led to the bashing, and we now have a picture of our external "I" being jumped by our fearful companions who are standing there seeing their own external "I"s lying in the bloody dust.

If we are smart and have the ability to use language to paint pretty pictures in the recall running through the minds of our companions, we might just be able to save ourselves. If we know that our companions are receiving neuronic impacts as a result of forming a picture of their external "I"s lying on the ground dead that conflict with the positive picture of their external "I"s contained in their intellectual "I"s, intellectual "I"s which are incapable of viewing the future as anything other than indefinite, and if we want to keep those neuronic impacts from driving our companions to jump on us and bash our own head in, we have to create a picture in their recall that shows their external "I"s safe and sound. After all, they too can only form a single picture in their recall, and if we can substitute a picture in their recall that does not cause neuronic impacts for the picture that is causing them neuronic impacts, then we can eliminate their neuronic impacts and quell what might well become our own lynching.

"He was plotting to kill us all!" we yell. "He told me that there was not enough fish to go around, and if I worked with him, the two of us could kill you all and have all the fish to ourselves."

The first impulse of our potential executioners is to laugh at the improbability of it all, the humor resulting from the sudden creation of an unexpected picture of the dead man trying to kill them.

But we persist: "He wanted me to lead you over to the edge of the creek and then he was going to sneak up behind you and hit you with that log over there."

We point vaguely in the direction of a log lying on the ground.

Faced with two opposing pictures, being killed by us and almost being killed by the dead man, and not knowing which one to put in recall because neither has support in reality, the laughter stops. Our companions are beginning to form a picture of a possibility, of our tormentor tormenting them.

This isn't hard to do because we weren't the only ones he had mouthed off to.

"If it wasn't for me," we finally cry, "that would be you lying there!"

We are leaving the external "I"s of each of our companions right where they had been, lying on the ground in a pool of blood but with the recall of our companions now showing the dead man alive as the reason they would be lying there dead. With us now as the savior who killed the scumbag who would have caused them to be lying there in a pool of blood, we are now the reason they no longer have to picture themselves lying there dead and thus the reason they no longer have to feel neuronic impacts.

The dead man is now a source of relief as the neuronic impacts stop, and our companions are now grateful to us for ending their pain, their fear.

This little drama is but one of an uncounted number that might play themselves out over the course of an emerging society, and the chance of it coming out so favorably are counterbalanced by the chance that it would come out badly. It still could come out badly if the dead man's relatives are proactive, in which case they might outtalk us or seek revenge on us, and then our relatives might seek to revenge their revenge, and their relatives might seek to revenge that revenge resulting in an endless cycle of revenge.

In an emerging society, if the society is to be successful, these dramas have to be resolved in a manner that will put them to rest as best they can be put to rest given the tracks they leave in reality.

What exactly are those tracks?

The body may well be dead and buried, but the event will live on in the recall of those who witnessed it and in the recall of those for whom a picture of the event has been created so that they too may have recall of the event.

The effect of that recall, the extent to which the recall produces neuronic impacts, or is even recalled more than once or twice, depends on the closeness of the mind with the recall to the subject of the recall and the nature of the interpretation of the neuronic impacts the recall produces.

First, the recall produces neuronic impacts because reality does not match recall!

We have a picture of someone in recall and there is no counterpart for that person in reality.

That person is dead and buried!

If we had formed all of our pictures of recall with that person in the picture, if we were the person's parents or his siblings, his lover or his children, then the hole in our recall would be constant, a hole in every picture we form of reality, for not only do we have a picture of self as an element of every picture of reality that we form, we have a picture of those around us.

If we meet someone only once or twice a year, then we have only a limited number of memory units in recall containing a picture of that person. If we grew up with someone, or someone grew up around us, we may have millions of memory units in recall containing a picture of that person.

We always have more than one element in the pictures we form in our recall. If we lived in a house, then the house would be an element of the pictures we formed when we were in the house. If we had a child that grew up in the house with us, then the pictures of the child we had in recall would also contain an element that was a picture of the house. If the child is all of a sudden gone, every picture of the house we form as we go around the house forming a picture of the house will have a hole in it, the element of the picture that was the child.

The hole in the picture, not agreeing with reality, produces neuronic impacts that we interpret as grief if we have no target to blame for the absence of the child in the picture, or revenge if we do have a target.

Even if we don't have a target for the pain a hole in our recall produces, we can manufacture one and put it in recall, and that target will be as real as if the target had left the tracks in reality that produced our loss.

Society cannot form without some sort of an arbiter that can objectively settle these dramas, bring them to a close in one way or another, because the basic purpose of society is the peaceful procurement of food, its peaceful consumption, a peaceful way to find shelter from the elements and a safe climate in which to produce and raise children.

But, if we do nothing without the prodding of neuronic impacts, and neuronic impacts require a conflict, where do the neuronic impacts come from that drive us to set up such an arbiter?

Empathy produces Golden Rule Behavior, the standards that tell us how we should behave, but empathy does not restrain our actions because we don't feel much empathy when we are responding to the pain of neuronic impacts.

There is another form of empathy required to prod us into giving up our freedom of action. We are driven to create an arbiter of our actions by the neuronic impacts produced by facing the consequences of our own actions in physical reality!

After our narrow escape, we would naturally replay the recall of the event, analyze the tracks we had laid down in physical reality, the events surrounding the bashing. We might well have mixed feelings when we recalled ourselves bashing in our tormentor's head.

We would naturally be happy with the absence of our tormentor because we had produced plenty of pictures in our recall of just such an absence.

But because recall is serial, because the elements of a picture can recall threads of thought which lead to other outcomes, we might also see ourselves as the result of a bad outcome, unable to alter the recall of our companions, and thus becoming the subject of their wrath.

We could just as easily see ourselves lying in the bloody dust with our tormentor, just as our companions had seen their own external "I"s lying in the bloody dust in place of our tormentor.

Instead of feeling good because we no longer had to recall our dead companion as a physical obstacle in reality, we might feel neuronic impacts as a result of forming recall of our external "I" lying dead in the dust. As a result of the pain, we would reflexively look around for the source of the neuronic impacts, a target against which we can seek revenge.

And we find only ourselves!

We picture ourselves lying in the dust, dead at the hands of our companions, but dead as a result of our own actions, the direct result of having bashed in our tormentor's head.

To say this presents a problem would be an understatement of immense proportions because we have no way to resolve our conflict and thus no way to get ourselves out of pain.

"If we hadn't killed our tormentor, then our external 'I' wouldn't be lying dead in the dust" becomes "if we hadn't killed our tormentor, I wouldn't be receiving these neuronic impacts."

The only way we can get rid of the pain of our neuronic impacts is to create a reality that doesn't exist, a reality that has our external "I" not having killed our tormentor.

But that reality not only doesn't exist in reality, it can never exist in reality. We have seen to that.

We have laid down tracks in physical reality that preclude it.

That reality can exist only in our recall.

We can never, ever again produce that reality because we have left our tracks in physical reality. We can never, ever again produce that reality because we have acted in reality and those acts in reality cannot be changed.

The neuronic impacts are coming from a conflict of an imagined recall, a picture of our external "I" not having acted, with a reality that cannot be changed, a picture of our external "I" having acted.

Our intellectual "I" is attempting to form a picture of our external "I" in recall that can never exist in physical reality because the acts of our external "I" in physical reality, acts performed as a result of our intellectual "I" forming a picture of our external "I" acting, have left tracks in physical reality, tracks that can never be changed.

Our intellectual "I" is being driven to form pictures of our external "I" engaging in acts which did not produce neuronic impacts at the time of the act, but are producing neuronic impacts when we recall the act.

Our intellectual "I" has allowed our external "I" to act in haste and now we are repenting at an endless leisure!

Our acts in reality are what morality is about. We might well have had a president who lusted in his heart, but lusting in one's heart is not an act in reality. Society might well want to limit heart-lusting to the extent possible under the assumption that it leads to real down and dirty lusting, acts in reality that society wants to prohibit, but there's not much society can do about lusting in recall.

Or is there?

When we are immersed in the neuronic impacts that result from wishing in our recall that we had not produced the picture that exists in reality, we are attempting to delimit the acts of our external "I"s. When we make a pact with ourselves not to act in a certain way in the future, we are simply attempting to avoid doing things that would cause us neuronic impacts in the future, actions we would regret after we performed them.

We are recognizing that our intellectual "I"s control the acts of our external "I"s because if our intellectual "I"s do not form a picture of our external "I"s engaging in the act, then our external "I"s can never engage in the act.

Seeing others in circumstances we would not ourselves wish to experience produces an objective standard of behavior, Golden Rule Behavior, but having an objective standard of behavior is not itself sufficient to restrain our actions in reality. It is the realization that we have an external "I" whose actions, if restrained, will relieve us from the pain of neuronic impacts in the future combined with the realization, acknowledged in our continued violations of Golden Rule Behavior, that we cannot ourselves restrain our actions, a fact based on the operation of our minds which evolved to allow us to continue to act, that leads us to willingly abdicate our freedom to act when those acts would cause us future pain.

As soon as we regret, as soon as we say, "I don't want my external 'I' doing something because I will feel bad about it later", the "I" defining the act needs to be an "I" separate and distinct from our positive intellectual "I"s which form naturally as a part of every picture of ourselves that we form as we move through physical reality because we can not ask a positive intellectual "I" that evolved to allow us to act in reality to limit our actions in reality!

The ability to judge the future adverse consequences of our acts to ourselves is the source of the societal "I".

We create a third "I", a ubiquitous "I", that represents the collective experience of society dealing with what acts we can engage in without later creating a conflict with our intellectual "I"s when we view our external "I"s engaged in the behavior, a conflict that would later cause us neuronic impacts, pain.

Acting together through experience, we create a ubiquitous "I" informed by a standard of behavior that reflects the collective experience of society concerning which acts will later cause us pain.

It is this ubiquitous "I" that is producing the neuronic impacts when we propose to act in ways that would cause us problems after we acted. The ubiquitous "I" has been programmed against acts the future recall of which will produce neuronic impacts. It produces a present conflict that will prevent us from engaging in acts that will cause us pain in the future.

The ubiquitous "I" is like random access memory in a computer. The acts it is programmed with, the acts that produce the neuronic impacts, can be any acts.

But, because the ubiquitous "I" is programmable doesn't make it any less the objective result of the mind's operation. It has to come into existence to compensate for the unintended by-product of the detector that evolved to move us through physical reality, the by-product that produces an awareness which can create realities that don't exist in physical reality.

We cannot bring our social interactions together to produce a society without some mechanism that would limit our behavior. The mechanism that regulates our behavior is not arbitrary and it is most certainly not the result of people sitting around the communal campfire saying one thing is bad and another is good.

The objective mechanism that arises to regulate our behavior and thus allows the social interactions that permit society to exist is the result of our collective recognition produced by the neuronic impacts we receive from our actions in reality, from the tracks we lay down in physical reality for all to see and react to, that there are some acts that produce neuronic impacts, not in others, but in ourselves, and that because our intellectual "I"s are the source of our actions, our intellectual "I"s have to be programmed to prevent us from forming some pictures to prevent us from engaging in the acts those pictures produce.

Our intellectual "I"s, however, only allow us to use experience to inform us how we, ourselves, should act.

The ubiquitous "I" that is created by society is a collective "I", an ideal "I", something that is behind our intellectual "I"s second guessing everything we allow our external "I"s to do in order to prevent us from acting when those actions would be against our own interests.

When our intellectual "I"s engage in a conversation with the ubiquitous "I" over how our external "I"s should behave, or more frequently, how our external "I"s should not have behaved, we are carrying on a conversation with something in reality for which we have no recall, and we associate it with the god we have created to explain the existence for which we can have no recall.

We create a word, morality, and place it in recall so that we will have something in recall to compare with the standards that have no apparent source in physical reality but which restrain our actions in physical reality.

Morality becomes Golden Rule Behavior, a part of the god that we use to explain our existence because we mistake it as something for which we can have no recall.

How does society program the ubiquitous "I" with Golden Rule Behavior?

5. HOW SOCIETY PROGRAMS THE UBIQUITOUS "I"

In *The Model Mind* I did not distinguish the ubiquitous "I" from the intellectual "I", instead creating what I referred to throughout the last half of the book as the idealistic "I" which is used as a hybrid moralistic intellectual "I". In that book I was concerned with how the mind, widely claimed to be nonexistent, an ethereal, perhaps philosophical concept could affect real physical matter in real physical reality. I was faced with the belief, born out of the denial that the mind existed, in an occult concept labeled consciousness supposedly generated by randomly connected neurons having no communication with the body other than through the operation of some ancient lizard-like brain core left over from prehistoric times which, through reams of arguments about predestination and free will, somehow either caused us to act in reality or caused us to respond to reality acting upon us, or some combination of the two, as a result of instinct, genetic predisposition, territorial imperative, or just plain orneriness, all ad hoc words used to label effects and therefore simulate comprehension.

And, of course, the fanatical belief in the nonexistence of the mind still prevails in a scientific community steeped in ignorance and superstition.

This is understandable!

Empirical science was structured to avoid the embarrassment of ever again having to admit to belief in a gross misperception like the pre-Copernican belief that the sun went around the Earth. It therefore made up rules that were designed to guard it against such a mistake. Having no idea what comprehension was, or how the mind operated, it decided that it would limit its realm of inquiry to what could be measured, the hard edges of physical reality.

To measure the hard edges of physical reality, empirical science had to devise detectors, telescopes, scales, probes, all feedback devices which could provide information about those hard edges. Because categorizing this information simulated comprehension, it gave us something to put in recall to match reality, empirical science established rules that required that questions about reality be mathematically measurable.

The most important questions about physical reality don't deal with the hard edges of that reality, however, but concern what those hard edges are doing in physical reality.

The most important questions about physical reality are those concerning what makes matter move in physical reality.

Because the force that makes matter move is not a hard edge in physical reality and therefore not directly measurable, is in fact measurable only by the way that it makes matter move, empirical science categorized questions of motion and force with questions of existence, abdicating explanations of force and motion to God. Thus, even though there is no basis for stating that objects fall as a result of a property of matter, gravity, other than believing that a spiritual entity installed gravity in matter when He or She created the universe, and certainly no basis for stating that objects move in a straight line other than believing that a spiritual entity installed straight-line motion in matter when He or She created the universe, this is what empirical science believes.

Immersed in the ignorance and superstition about physical reality that results from ignoring the basic questions about physical reality, why objects fall and why the sun comes up every day, totally obsessed with its desire to produce ever more complex and tenuous detectors to make ever more complex and tenuous measurements of the hard edges of physical reality, empirical science ignores the only detector we have to comprehend the questions of motion and force those hard edges present, our minds.

The rules that empirical science has created to control its analysis of physical reality exclude our analysis of the nature and operation of the mind and thus puts our analysis of how the mind operates to perceive reality beyond knowledge. As a quasi-religious institution, empirical science first makes up a bunch of stuff that forms a picture of how physical reality operates, looks for a missing element of the picture, a hole in the made-up stuff, and believes that if that hole in the picture, called a predictive fact, is found, then all the made-up stuff is actually reality.

Empirical science, believing that its fantasies can be proven by finding predictive facts, directs all of its resources to constructing abstruse detectors to find predictive facts so that its practitioners can delude themselves into believing that they understand force and motion and ignores the only detector we have to understand force and motion, the mind.

Although in discussing how the mind moved matter, *The Model Mind* required explaining temperament, the relationship between nature and nurture, and although it described a lot of behavior, it did not directly face the question of how moral behavior arises. In describing the existence of neuronic impacts, the electrical currents generated by the brain that operate the mind and which enter the body when the mind ceases to operate as a result of recall and reality disagreeing, the nature part of the mechanism, it became apparent that the extent to which an organism responded to the neuronic impacts would control how the organism behaved in reality. The genetic response to pain is certainly nature, but the way the organism is taught to treat that pain, or the way the organism interprets that pain, is the nurture part.

Someone born with subsystems as tough as old shoe leather might never be concerned with the neuronic impacts he or she receives. Individuals who because of genetic inheritance, feel little pain, would be unexcitable in youth and daredevils in adulthood. Individuals who because of genetic inheritance, have little tolerance for pain, would be excitable in youth and withdrawn as adults.

Of course, the vast majority of individuals would fall in the great "in-between" with average responses to pain.

A low pain resistant individual could be schooled to endure vast amounts of pain while a high pain resistant individual could be berated into abject submission. A high pain resistant individual could learn to get sympathy by mimicking pain, while a low pain resistant individual could be the source of such emotional and physical outbursts that people shied away, turning him into an unchallenged bully.

A low pain resistant Prince could become a tyrant while a high pain resistant King could rule with equanimity.

Temperament is a contest between our intellectual and external "I"s carried out by the roll of the societal dice with respect to position played out against the strength of our subsystems to resist the pain of neuronic impacts. It provides the backdrop for behavior, which is the conscious decision to act or not act in a certain way.

The conscious decision to act or not act in a certain way is made when our intellectual "I", our concept of self cycled into our recall at any particular time, makes decisions with respect to how our external "I" is going to act by comparing various courses of action with both the experience of our intellectual "I" and with a template provided by society, the morality programmed into the ubiquitous "I", by the relative pain the neuronic impacts produced by the comparison creates.

Society has an interest in programming our intellectual "I"s because it has an interest in protecting itself against potential acts in reality arising from our ability to recall a reality that does not exist and thus a reality beyond its reach. Society has an interest in this ability to create recall that doesn't exist in reality because recall is the source of all actions in reality.

Any act can be cobbled together in recall and thus any act can be attempted in reality!

Society has an overriding interest in controlling the acts of its members because it is only by limiting the scope of permissible behavior that its members can come together to form a society.

Society coalesces around two truths: All of its members can recognize the need for Golden Rule Behavior, a need that arises from empathy, and all of its members experience regret for actions that violate Golden Rule Behavior.

This regret has a solid basis in the pain of neuronic impacts.

It is the fear of fear!

When we stood over our dead tormentor with our living companions looking first at the dead body and then at us, putting together a picture of us making them as dead as our tormentor, we unrolled our silver tongue because we could picture our companions making us as dead as our tormentor.

We all had common neuronic impacts and we interpreted them as fear.

When we form a picture of our external "I"s in recall dead, the resulting picture opposes the normal positive picture our intellectual "I"s have of our external "I"s moving safely through physical reality.

The neuronic impacts are very basic.

We have two conditions with respect to the electrical flows that operate our bodies.

When our minds cannot compare recall and reality, we receive neuronic impacts that are subject to interpretation, but in their most consistent form result in anger, or if massive, rage.

However, when we face the unfaceable, we are dealing with the set of electrical flows that operate our bodies, that move our physical bodies through physical reality. When we are facing our death, our nonexistence, our minds shut down altogether and we don't even receive the electric flows that maintain our bodies with respect to physical reality.

Massive neuronic impacts result in rage but the absence of neuronic impacts is mind stopping, body paralyzing fear.

The pain we feel when facing death involves our nonexistence and can eliminate the electric flows maintaining our body's position while at the same time causing massive neuronic impacts!

The purpose of our minds is to move us through external reality.

External reality exists.

We exist in external reality.

We find it impossible to understand that empty space is just that, empty, because our minds evolved to form a picture of something, not nothing. If we try to form a picture of nothing, then we can have no recall because recall is recall of something.

We create a space and time that are quantities when space and time have no independent existence simply because we are evolutionarily disabled from not recalling something.

When we try to picture nothing, we are trying to picture something for which we have no recall and we feel uncomfortable. We have trouble holding a thought of no recall in recall.

When we think of our own death, our demise, we are thinking of our nonexistence, nothing. We simply can't visualize it. We can form recall with ourselves not present and produce a will to provide for our heirs, but we are still producing recall, of the will if not of our external "I"s making the will.

But we have difficulty thinking of ourselves as not there, not existing.

Because our very existence is produced by the serial recall of pictures of ourselves, we have a picture of ourselves in recall at all times. We can't recall without recalling a picture of ourselves so it is difficult to recall a picture of ourselves not existing.

Thus, when we stand around a dead body and picture ourselves dead, we are creating the most basic of mental conflicts, a disagreement of recall with reality that goes to the very concept of self that is basic to recall, our existence, and the neuronic impacts our paralyzed bodies receive are profound indeed.

We feel a fear that eats at the soul of our existence!

Society understands this fear quite well. After all, society is composed of ourselves.

Society may not understand that the fear is the result of neuronic impacts, the electrical shocks to the subsystems that are produced when our minds attempt to form two opposing pictures because its scientific sycophants don't recognize that there is a mind, they don't recognize that electrical currents physically exist, they don't recognize that those currents can flow from one place to another in the body, and they don't know that those electrical currents can disrupt the communications between the various subsystems to result in physical pain.

Society doesn't have to understand.

We feel uncomfortable when we produce recall of our external "I"s being killed because the recall forces us to recall our nonexistence, something that conflicts profoundly with our positive intellectual "I"s.

This is all society has to understand.

Society has absolutely no problem figuring out how to program our intellectual "I"s so that we have an independent ubiquitous "I" which provides a template for our intellectual "I"s to use in forming possible courses of action for our external "I"s.

Society programs the ubiquitous "I" by carrying out vicarious punishments on our external "I"s for violations of the prohibitions that define Golden Rule Behavior!

Without punishment, there can be no morality because without examples in our recall of our external "I"s being punished for violations of the prohibitions that define Golden Rule Behavior we will not experience neuronic impacts when we form a picture of ourselves violating the prohibitions, and thus, with the absence of pain, Golden Rule Behavior will become undefined.

Morality is the limitation of behavior society defines by the acts it is willing to punish. If society does not want public conjugation between consenting adults, it will punish couples it finds to be engaged in public conjugation. If it ceases to punish couples for engaging in public conjugation, then such acts cease to define morality.

Just as there can be no morality without neuronic impacts, there can be no morality without punishment because it is the prospect of punishment that produces neuronic impacts.

Punishment defines morality!

We are still simply matter animated in physical reality. How does programming the intellectual "I" with the ubiquitous "I" containing societal dictates control an organism's actions in physical reality?

Our minds evolved to move us safely through physical reality. Before we can act in physical reality, we have to form a picture of our external "I"s acting in our recall. We are able to form a picture of physical reality because the current flows produced by our senses form a representation of the hard edges of reality in our minds. At the same time, these electrical currents recall memory units stored in our recall that contain similar pictures of reality. These recalled pictures have an added element. They contain the evolutionary "I"s, our intellectual "I"s which generate the self by its viewpoint of physical reality and our external "I"s which have been produced by experience, by actually moving through that physical reality.

This recall also contains the ubiquitous "I", an objective template dealing with how we should behave.

If we are trying to move through a physical reality for which we have no recall, we do not have anything to match with the picture of physical reality that we are forming in our mind. As a result, we travel through that reality safari style, sending out scouts in advance of our arrival. We reverse the process of recalling a picture of our external "I"s moving through physical reality and focus on physical reality, testing pictures of our external "I"s in that physical reality to make sure we don't fall off of a cliff or get swept away by a raging current.

But when we have trod the path before, we don't have to focus on physical reality to move through that physical reality. The physical reality produces a serial recall that shows our external "I"s with respect to that physical reality.

The only thing that would stop our recall process is if a picture of physical reality attempted to form in our minds that did not match the serial recall already passing through our minds.

For instance, if we are walking the trodden path and a space ship lands in front of us, the shock of reality not matching recall will stop our muscles from moving us smoothly through reality causing us to stop short. The pause will give us time to search our recall to come up with something that matches what we now see in reality. If we can't get something in recall that matches what we see, we will stay stopped.

However, when we are traveling the trodden path, with no surprises, nothing that would produce neuronic impacts that would call our attention to changed reality, we are forming pictures of our external "I"s that do not exist in reality, that are slightly ahead of our progress on the path.

We have to have a picture of ourselves acting in reality in order to act in reality.

It is only when reality does not agree with recall that the mind is stopped from operating and neuronic impacts enter the wet works of our bodies to disrupt our subsystems.

This is the mechanism that allows our minds to be aware of changes in external reality. Just as our minds operate by exception, notifying our bodies of changed reality by ceasing to operate and sending electrical flows into the subsystems to shock those subsystems so that we can no longer act, *if our minds are incapable of operating, if we are incapable of forming a picture of ourselves acting in physical reality, we will not be able to act in physical reality.*

When our minds are not operating, we cannot form a picture of our external "I"s acting in physical reality and when our minds are not forming a picture of our external "I"s acting in physical reality, then our bodies are not going anywhere.

If our minds do not form a picture of our external "I"s acting, then we are not going to act.

All society has to do is keep our minds from forming pictures of our external "I"s acting in physical reality and we will not act in physical reality!

Society programs our intellectual "I"s with moral strictures that create a core "I", the ubiquitous "I", that then becomes a template for our behavior. The neuronic impacts produced by trying to form a picture of our external "I"s engaged in acts that violate the template for Golden Rule Behavior prevents us from forming the picture of our external "I"s acting, and thus prevents us from acting.

The ten commandments codify Golden Rule Behavior. Using the old testament version, after the first four commandments, which are designed to protect the source of the authority generating the prohibitions, and the fifth commandment, which is designed to protect the parents, the immediate authority, the representative of society for programming the ubiquitous "I" into children, the remaining five commandments deal with acts prohibited in reality. These acts are basic to the operation of society, don't kill, don't commit adultery, don't steal, don't lie or form recall relating to adultery or stealing other people's property.

Today, when there are perhaps two thousand different Federal crimes and tens of thousands of regulatory prohibitions that evoke criminal penalties, when it is prohibited to do such unspecific things as making terrorist threats, interfering in governmental operations or with the administration of government, disrupting the operation of a school or using a weapon of mass destruction, and such specific things as writing a check for under a dollar, when clear laws are used for unintended purposes, a photographer blocking a movie star to get a picture jailed for kidnapping or a family convicted of murder when their dogs jump the back fence, the simple "Thou-shalt-nots" of the biblical injunctions should stand out loud and clear.

A successful society programs the ubiquitous "I" by painting a clear picture of the conduct it wishes to prohibit. Only police states make the number of crimes both uncountable and indescribable in clear picture format so that any member of the society is at risk of prosecution for any crime and random acts give rise to multiple charges.

Police states proliferate laws because they maintain their power by fear, the same fear that society associates with the acts it seeks to prohibit by preventing our intellectual "I"s from forming a picture of our external "I"s engaged in those acts.

Taking the clear prohibition against murder, using the old testament punishment of an eye for an eye, and focusing on public executions in the town square, we can connect the neuronic impacts that are produced when we visualize our external "I"s going under the ax with the violations of Golden Rule Behavior society desires to prohibit.

Those that equate the immorality of violating the societal prohibition against taking a life with society taking a life to instill in its members the immorality of taking a life are understandably ignorant of the true purpose of punishing violations of the prohibitions that define Golden Rule Behavior.

The purpose of punishment is to create recall that is stored at the same electrical charge as the acts the punishment seeks to prohibit. Creating recall that is stored at the same current level takes advantage of the mind's operation that allows us to recall a tree when we see a tree. If we store a picture of ourselves having our head chopped off with a picture of ourselves taking another's life, when we form a picture of ourselves taking another's life in order to take a life, we will immediately recall a picture of our head being chopped off.

When events in reality drive us to produce recall of ourselves engaging in actions that violate Golden Rule Behavior, the current level created by the picture of ourselves violating Golden Rule Behavior will recall the punishment for the violation, the picture of our external "I"s being punished will conflict with the positive picture our intellectual "I"s have of our external "I"s, and we will receive neuronic impacts that will prevent us from acting.

We will simply cease to function from base fear!

Society produces public punishments for violations of Golden Rule Behavior so that we will place our external "I"s in place of those being punished and thus store the consequences of the violations of Golden Rule Behavior with the violations of Golden Rule Behavior.

The process that society uses to program the ubiquitous "I" is quite simple.

First there has to be a prohibited act defined by Golden Rule Behavior.

Second, there has to be a transgression, a violation of Golden Rule Behavior.

Third, there has to be a clear picture of punishment.

Fourth, there has to be a clear connection between the act for which the punishment is prescribed and the punishment.

Fifth, there has to be clear picture of the punishment being administered on the person who violated Golden Rule Behavior. If the picture of the punishment is not clear, then our intellectual "I"s can not visualize our external "I"s being the subject of the punishment.

Sixth, the punishment has to occur with reasonable proximity to the act for which the punishment is being administered. Delaying the punishment for acts society seeks to prohibit only promotes the commission of those acts because our intellectual "I"s cannot see a clear picture of our external "I"s being punished when the punishment is interminably delayed.

Taking the prohibitions against acting that define the morality of the ten commandments, we can see the ubiquitous "I", the moral intellectual "I", being formed. When we see individual members of society losing an eye for taking an eye or losing a tooth for taking a tooth, the same empathy that produces Golden Rule Behavior exerts itself.

Our recall function pictures our external "I"s being punished and we receive neuronic impacts.

Any subsequent attempt to form a picture that involves violating one of the societal prohibitions will recall the punishment and produce neuronic impacts.

We start to stick someone's eye out and we recall our own eye being stuck out!

We do not willingly form pictures that cause us pain and we can't form a picture that paralyzes us with fear.

Thus, we will not willingly form a picture that involves ourselves violating societal prohibitions.

We can only act if we form a picture of our external "I"s acting so that society protects itself by preventing us from acting in violation of societal prohibitions by using our own neuronic impacts to prevent us from forming pictures of ourselves committing the violations.

However, we violate the prohibitions of Golden Rule Behavior all the time. The ubiquitous "I" is a template for behavior which may or may not prevent our acts. Because our mind formed to allow us to act unless we are faced with obstacles in reality, and morality is not an obstacle in reality, the programming of a ubiquitous "I" to attempt to control our actions in reality raises the question of free will. Questions of free will require an analysis of how our intellectual "I"s make decisions.

As we walk down the street and turn a corner, we might run smack into some oversized slob. As we pick ourselves up out of the mud puddle, we are more surprised than anything else because we haven't as yet been able to form a clear picture of what happened. We do know that we were happily moving along in physical reality, our recall forming a picture of our external "I" moving through that reality ruminating on our relationship with our one true love, and the next thing we know, we don't have a picture of ourselves moving, we have a picture of the sky above and the mud below.

The conflict of reality, the mud bath, with recall, our external "I" moving freely through physical reality ruminating on our one true love sends neuronic impacts into our body. We look around to see what circumstances in physical reality have changed to produce our neuronic impacts. We see the big pile of dog diddle we collided with and we start to interpret the neuronic impacts as anger. Our external "I" has been wronged and being wronged contradicts the positive picture of our external "I" embodied in our intellectual "I" which is filled with concern for the condition of our external "I" and the resulting conflict increases the neuronic impacts.

However, the recall of our external "I" being wronged is interrupted by a picture of the big bruiser's face wrinkled in deep concern, apologetic noises streaming out of his mouth as he leans over, lifts us bodily from the mud puddle, dirtying himself as he tries to clean us up, profusely offering to pay for our cleaning in the process.

The friendly hulk's concern for our external "I" agrees with the concern of our own intellectual "I" for our external "I" and the agreement forms a picture of our external "I" in good hands, being taken care of by the person that caused the accident.

The conflict disappears, the neuronic impacts stop and our anger dissipates.

In fact, we start to feel pretty good, even grateful.

On the other hand, the big bruiser might start screaming at us, kick some dust in the mud puddle to create more mud, blame us for the whole thing and go on his way.

Now we have recall that includes our external "I" ending up in a mud puddle and recall that includes our intellectual "I" being responsible for our external "I" ending up in the mud puddle, an awfully hard picture to form because it opposes the positive picture our intellectual "I" must have of our external "I" moving in reality, and this on top of the real picture our intellectual "I" has of our external "I" being mistreated.

The cause of the accident may well be in doubt, but this subsequent treatment is a reality, and every time we recall the subsequent treatment, the proverbial sand kicked in our eyes, we will extend the blame and the desire for revenge created by the neuronic impacts to the original accident.

As the guy bullies off, leaving us to stew in our juices, we vow revenge. We follow him to his lair, holding back, hiding out of sight lest he become aware of us. We don't want to cause him neuronic impacts from picturing his own external "I" being slaughtered by us in the darkness of night because that might lead to his cleaning our clock before we have a chance to clean his.

Knowing now where he waters, we go home to sharpen our knife.

As the grinding wheel turns, we recall pictures of our disgrace and those pictures create intense agony as a result of the ensuing neuronic impacts.

We bear down on the grinding wheel to use up the unwanted electrons that are flooding our body

We try and think of our one true love to stop the neuronic impacts, but thinking of her at the same time that we are trying not to think of our disgrace only puts her in recall as a witness to our disgrace, increasing our agony.

We substitute pictures of the big bruiser being forced to grovel in the mud at our feet and the recall ameliorates our neuronic impacts.

In fact, holding a picture in recall of our tormentor in agony allows us to take the knife we are grinding to a brilliant sharpness and conduct all sorts of creative configurations on his body in our recall. The longer we can keep pictures of ourselves slicing and dicing our tormentor in recall, the longer we can keep the pictures of our own humiliation out of our recall and the longer we can stave off our own pain.

Visualizing revenge replaces pictures of our disgrace and eliminates our neuronic impacts giving us the pleasure of surcease.

The absence of the sharp neuronic impacts created by picturing our own misfortune is a distinct pleasure and avoiding the neuronic impacts, seeking pleasure, drives us to continually form a picture of our tormentor being tormented by our external "I".

We blissfully finish sharpening the knife, having dissipated a lot of the excess electrons disrupting our body in the process, and we head for the door. With all of the pictures in recall of the acts we are going to carry out on our tormentor, the absence of our tormentor now produces neuronic impacts. Because we are now taking action, however, our recall function starts to serially recall the steps our external "I" will take to accomplish our final goal. A picture of the final goal comes into recall. We see our tormentor groveling at our feet, in the throes of death, our knife in hand, blood dripping down upon our shoes.

Our intellectual "I" is immediately replaced with the ubiquitous "I" which carries a picture of the consequences of committing the act of murder.

The ubiquitous "I" forms a picture of our external "I" in the town square with our hands tied behind our back, an ax descending swiftly upon the back of our neck.

The neuronic impacts are immediate and overpowering!

Our legs grow weak and we might even stop in our tracks, unable to proceed to our destiny.

The ubiquitous "I" stores the act and the punishment at the same current level. That is why the picture of the act and the punishment have to be clear, connected and contemporary. The ubiquitous "I" lies dormant in the wet works of the brain until a picture of the external "I" committing the act is forced into recall in response to actual or recalled reality. The picture of the external "I" engaging in the act, stored at the same current level as the consequences of engaging in the act, recall those consequences.

The recall of the consequences, a negative picture of the external "I", then causes neuronic impacts by conflicting with the positive picture the intellectual "I" has of the external "I".

Now our intellectual "I" has three pictures that can be recalled dealing with proposed courses of action that we can test against our intellectual "I" as informed by the ubiquitous "I", the societal template, to compare the extent to which each will produce neuronic impacts and thus experience how each makes us feel.

The first picture is of our external "I" being humiliated, the original disgrace, which produces neuronic impacts.

The second picture is of our external "I" killing our tormentor, which doesn't produce neuronic impacts, and, in fact, produces pleasure, the relief from neuronic impacts.

The third picture is of our external "I" being executed, which causes us profound neuronic impacts.

The second picture always produces the third, so the question is whether the neuronic impacts of the third picture can turn the neuronic impacts of the first picture into background noise so that the first picture can never become a reality.

This is the free will philosophers and empiricists have been claiming for years doesn't exist.

We judge what we are going to do by comparing the level of neuronic impacts produced by creating pictures of our external "I"s engaged in alternate courses of action. The societal prohibitions programmed into the ubiquitous "I" serve to increase the level of the neuronic impacts when a proposed course of action violates one of those prohibitions, making it harder for us to maintain a picture in recall of our external "I"s actually performing those acts.

We picture our tormentor dead.

We receive neuronic impacts.

We picture ourselves on the chopping block.

We receive neuronic impacts.

Because we can hold a picture of our external "I"s in recall longer the less neuronic impacts the picture creates, the picture of our external "I"s producing the least neuronic impacts will probably end up being the picture that becomes a reality, the picture on which we act.

On the other hand, even though seeing our external "I"s on the chopping block causes us intolerable neuronic impacts, we might exercise our free will and just say, the hell with it, we'll talk our way out of it afterwards.

And we just might!

However, violating the dictates of the ubiquitous "I", instead of freeing our will, can lead to further restrictions on our freedom of action because it boxes in our free will with neuronic impacts.

6. THE EXERCISE OF FREE WILL

The only limitation we have on our free will, our ability to act in physical reality, is our inability to form and hold in our recall a picture of our external "I"s acting in physical reality.

A major limitation on our ability to hold in our recall a picture of our external "I"s acting in physical reality is the pain neuronic impacts produce when the picture of our external "I"s acting opposes our concept of self, either centered in our intellectual "I"s, the sum total of our experience, of having our fingers burned in the past or centered in the ubiquitous "I", the morality society programs into our recall. This limitation prevents us from forming a picture in our minds because the picture produces too much pain.

While experience is a great teacher, the programming of the ubiquitous "I" involves an attempt on the part of society to prevent us from acting by preventing us from forming a picture of ourselves acting where that picture of ourselves acting is a response to the temptations of physical reality.

It is fairly simple to not form a picture of our external "I"s sticking our hand on a hot burner when we have been burned before.

When it comes to the "Thou-shalt-nots", however, the behavior that society is attempting to prohibit is actually behavior that is desirable to the person recalling it. We see the ring on the finger of our neighbor's wife and we want it. We see our neighbor's wife and we want her.

Instead of not forming a picture of ourselves acting, we have to eliminate a picture of ourselves acting!

There is a limitation on society's ability to program the ubiquitous "I" to prevent us from acting when the source of the pictures that provide the basis for our actions are biological, built into our subsystems, a result of our body's evolved purposes.

The limitation of society's ability to prevent us from acting by preventing us from forming a picture of our external "I"s acting in physical reality arises when our bodies produce recall that breaks the connection between our proposed acts and societal prohibitions by recalling an intellectual "I" that was not in recall when the programming occurred, when the ubiquitous "I" was installed in recall. Because our minds are capable of forming only a single picture at a time, the intellectual "I" that represents the current level at which the prohibitions of the ubiquitous "I" are stored may not be available when the opportunity to commit the violations arises.

We know there is a connection between our acts and societal prohibitions but the current level recalling our proposed act is too strong to permit recall of the punishment. The connection between the behavior and the prohibition produces a ghost of the intellectual "I" that was in recall when the prohibition was programmed into us but it can only look on in horror, too weak to influence the onrush of biological necessity.

If the societal prohibitions that make up the ubiquitous "I" are associated with recall that is stored at a current level which is out of range when the prohibited acts present themselves, then the intellectual "I" that is making the decisions concerning what the external "I" will do will not be restrained by societal prohibitions because the proposed actions will not recall the societal prohibitions with sufficient clarity to create a conflict that would produce sufficient pain to interfere with the proposed pleasure.

When physical needs, hunger or sex, produce specific pictures of a juicy roast or an even juicier neighbor, our physical needs keep the picture fixed in recall and nothing prevents us from forming the pictures of our external "I"s doing whatever comes to mind.

The latter limitation, physical necessity, leads to a lot of violations of the former limitation, societal dictates!

Society cannot program us against sexual behavior when our sexual intellectual "I"s are in recall because, besides being counterproductive to the purpose of prohibiting behavior, it would be impossible to get our attention. As a result, when our sexual intellectual "I"s are in recall, there are no societal prohibitions.

If we lose the battle between the pictures of proper and improper behavior the ubiquitous "I" attempts to form in our recall to exotic pictures of the possible, the temptations of the flesh continually forced into our recall, then we will end up with a whole lot of experience that's painful to recall.

Even though the pain neuronic impacts produce results in a battleground as to which pictures of our external "I"s acting in physical reality we end up being comfortable forming, and therefore how we end up acting in physical reality, when the ubiquitous "I" is not in recall we are free to act any way we wish!

The reality of free will is evidenced by our every day movements through physical reality.

We make choices in everything that we do.

However, because there has been no way to connect the choices we make to the mind, in fact, no recognition that there even is a mind, or a consciousness, the self that the mind generates, and thus nothing in reality to chose between one course action and another course of action, free will has been analogized to things for which we can have no recall.

We have already seen what happens when we have things for which we can have no recall. When we contemplate the source of our existence, the source of the existence of even a single bit of matter, we can have no recall, and we have no recourse against the neuronic impacts that result from having nothing in recall with which to match reality but to produce something in recall, a name, a god, a conceptual entity to match the reality for which we can have no recall.

We can never understand the god we create, but that is the point. We create a god to produce recall that will make us believe that we understand.

When pictures that seek to prohibit our actions pop into our minds as a result of being programmed with "Thou-shalt-nots", we have no idea what is attempting to restrain our actions. When we feel pain as a result of attempting to contemplate acts that violate the prohibitions that define Golden Rule Behavior, and we have no recall for the source of that pain, we do what we have learned has worked in the past.

We make up a word!

We create the nebulous term morality.

We have no recall connecting the mental processes that dictate our inability to act to the societal programming and only a dim recognition of the programming, so we associate the morality we live by with our creator, the god that made the matter that makes us up.

When we fail to establish a physical explanation for why we are moral animate matter, why we behave in a certain manner, why we fail to act when those acts would only hurt, on an immediate basis, others and not ourselves, we have abdicated the answer to the question of how behavior arises, questions dealing with our ability to act or not act in reality according to our own lights, to the area of existence for which we can have no recall, to the religious or occult.

And we have consigned free will to the same realm.

There is, however, only one thing for which we can have no recall, only one thing for which we can not come up with a mechanical explanation dealing with process, and that is the creation of matter itself.

The list of the facts in physical reality whose explanation we have abdicated to the occult is limitless, including the word "gravity" to abdicate comprehension for why objects fall, the words "angular momentum" to abdicate comprehension for why planets rotate, the words "swirling mass of gas" to abdicate comprehension for why planets orbit, the words "a moving charge" to abdicate comprehension for electricity, the words "analogous to water waves" to abdicate comprehension for light and the words "molecular magnets" to abdicate comprehension for what makes magnets move.

So it shouldn't be too much of a surprise to find ourselves abdicating our comprehension when it comes to understanding the nature of the free will we exercise every day to the words "neural network" to disguise our ignorance of the existence of a self capable of making choices.

Because we have abdicated our responsibility to comprehend free will and consigned it to the realms of philosophy and religion, we are able to say that the exercise of our free will is actually an illusion, that every thing we do is predetermined by the same god to which we have abdicated the explanation for both our existence and the motion in our existence.

As a result, when we are exercising free will, when we are actually using the process of testing alternative courses of action to judge the pain the recalled acts produce, when we are making choices, we are not actually exercising free will, we are not actually making choices, we are simply responding to choices made for us by our god or occult neural networks.

But we know that we make choices, and with the exercise of a little of the mental power empirical science denies exists, we can figure out that we exercise free will by forming a picture of ourselves acting and then judging the compatibility of the proposed courses of action by the neuronic impacts the proposed acts produce with the picture of our self, our intellectual "I"s already existing in recall, the picture of self that is generated by the recall that always has a picture of the point of view that is generating the picture as an element of the pictures it is generating.

The fact that our recall generates a self, a viewpoint, eliminates the universal objection to the existence of free will, the objection that there is nothing that can make the choices inherent in free will.

When we evolve to the point that we can form pictures of reality in our recall when reality is not present, our recall produces the point of view that can make choices by forming alternate pictures of our external "I"s engaging in different courses of action and then comparing those alternate courses of action by the neuronic impacts they produce when they conflict with the viewpoint informed by experience and societal dictates.

The fact that different courses of action produce different degrees of neuronic impacts eliminates the objection to free will that there is no objective basis for making decisions about how we should act.

We would not form pictures of ourselves jumping off a cliff because the neuronic impacts would be too painful.

We would not form pictures of ourselves murdering someone when we know the consequences will be the same as jumping off of a cliff, our untimely end.

Our intellectual "I"s, to the extent that they are informed by the societal constraints of the ubiquitous "I", make a choice to act or not to act simply by maintaining a picture of our external "I"s acting in physical reality, a requirement before our actions can become a reality or, because of the level of neuronic impacts proposed courses of action produce, because of the pain the pictures produce, abandoning the recall of our external "I"s acting in physical reality and thus eliminating the chance of our external "I"s taking action because we can not act in furtherance of abandoned recall.

Some of our choices are quite basic. If we are lying abed, comfortable, falling in and out of random recall in the form of dreams, we might feel like lying abed forever.

If we attempt to lie abed forever, however, we will eventually burn off enough heat in the form of electrons, energy, that our subsystems will need to replenish themselves if they are to continue to operate in conjunction with one another. When our subsystems need energy, they communicate with our central source of energy, our stomachs. Our stomachs, being continually polled for energy, will eventually run out of the ability to answer the poll, ceasing to provide energy to our subsystems. The polling of our subsystems will become more insistent, and the bombardment of these electronic messages on our stomachs will eventually produce a physical effect which is communicated to our minds.

In creatures simpler than ourselves, these signals would result in the direct and ceaseless movement of the organism in search of food. However, with our sophisticated ability to form pictures of reality when reality is not present, we would have long since stored memory units associated with the level of current produced by our stomach as it started producing hunger pangs. Our recall might take the shape of a huge steak, a dish of ice cream or anything else that has proven to satisfy our hunger in the past.

Empirical science, denying any connection between our minds and our bodies, mindlessly concludes that our hunger pains, generated by our empty stomachs, drive our bodies to seek out sustenance through a connection with a left-over primitive reptilian instinct buried beneath layers and layers of evolutionary development at the core of the wet works of the brain.

When we ask, well, where is this reptilian anachronism, empirical science, in much the same way that it points to a blur of light on a photographic plate and says: "See, there's a whole slew of stars being formed and thus we are seeing the remnants of the big bang and the beginning of time!" can produce an actual picture of the brain with a little dot on a nondescript picture of cellular swirls and swatches and say: "See, there's the reptilian brain that controls all of our actions and here is its location, and that settles that!"

According to empirical science's occult and esoteric system, the body communicates chemically through the central nervous system with the reptilian brain stem which then coordinates action within the body. If we are attacked, our bodies release massive amounts of adrenalin which activates our muscles to instinctively move us through reality, flee the attack, or fight the attacker. Salivating to hunger pains is just a Pavlovian reaction modulated by the brain stem, which, encased in its leathery skin, releases secretions here and there that allow the body to respond this way or that in response to one or another of the provocations provided by physical reality.

While all of this is going on beneath the neck, the neurons are sitting above the fray randomly making connections about what is going on, and those random connections, with the aid of something called chemical messengers, flitter thither and hither, generating the consciousness which, being but a mirage, has no independent ability to control what is going on below.

All of this is quite senseless, but to hide the senselessness, empirical science is quick to exclaim loud and long: "What a complex and marvelous system the brain is, the most intricate structure in the universe, one quite beyond the realm of human understanding!" which, by this expressed ignorance, effectively consigns the mind to the realm of whatever god we happen to believe in.

In fact, which means, in the real world in which our physical bodies exist, just as our subsystems are subjected to current flows, either in the form of specifically directed current flows that move whatever muscles have to be moved in order to conform our bodies to the picture we have constructed of our external "I"s in physical reality or in the form of neuronic impacts that invade our subsystems to warn us of changes in physical reality so that we don't proceed to walk off the edge of cliffs, so do our subsystems produce current flows that enter our minds and, because the flows contain a charge, cause our minds to generate current flows that recall memory units, pictures of reality stored in our neuronic storage bins, pictures which match the current levels entering our minds.

We "see" pictures from our eyes because the eyes collect different current flows which all register as different current levels in the mind, the individual elements of the pictures making up a total current level at which the memory units containing the pictures are stored.

Touch, hearing, taste and smell do not, like the eyes which transmit actual information about the locations of the hard edges of physical reality for reconstruction in the mind, represent current flows that can establish the pattern in our minds that we see as a picture. Current levels from these four sources can, however, recall a picture which has been stored at the unique current level of the senses. We might well associate a loud crashing noise with a falling tree and recall a picture of a falling tree when we hear a loud crashing noise. We might also associate the smell of warm butter with the picture of a baking cake and recall a picture of a baking cake when we smell warm butter.

Language is merely the process of connecting the current level at which a word is stored with the current level at which the picture the word represents is stored so that we have comparison, and thus comprehension when we hear the word. A string of words creates serial recall which, because it places actions in the context of time, structures the syntax we develop to order the words.

In like manner, nonspecific current levels generated by our body's subsystems can become associated with specific pictures as we experience the sensations that produce the nonspecific currents. Our bodies are not passive responders to our mind's electrical communications, but rather a partner in communication, keeping our minds aware not only where each part of our body is in relation to the pictures our minds are forming of external reality, but giving our mind a status check on the condition of each of our body parts. Primitive animate matter might well move away from heat because of sensors that communicate directly with its motor responses, just as our bodies have retained this strategy to move a finger out of a burning flame without our bodies communicating through the wet works of our brains. But because we can form and store pictures of physical reality, and recall those picture when physical reality is not present, we can see the fire, feel its heat, and recall a picture of what will happen if we go too close to the fire because we have been too close, or have seen someone else go too close or have had a picture of someone else going too close painted in vivid language for us so that we can associate the heat with the picture.

Our stomachs send current flows to our minds which cause our minds to recall pictures of our external "I"s eating, our bladders and bowels send current flows to our minds which cause our minds to recall pictures of our external "I"s evacuating and our reproductive organs send current flows to our minds which cause our minds to recall pictures of our external "I"s engaging in reproductive acts.

We can also recall pictures of our external "I"s eating, evacuating and procreating without actually doing so in external reality, and in the process trick our various subsystems into responding appropriately, the picture of a big slice of chocolate cake creating hunger pangs, the sound of a running faucet creating the urge to go to the bathroom and the recall of the sex act sending us tumbling into the nearest bed.

So when we are lying abed enjoying our languid dreams, our hunger pangs will eventually cause some of our dreams to take the form of bacon and eggs.

As soon as we have a picture of bacon and eggs in our recall, we have a conflict with reality because there are no bacon eggs in reality. If we are going to produce a reality that matches our recall, the bacon and eggs that exist only in our recall, then we are going to have to get up and make the bacon and eggs.

As long as we recall bacon and eggs and there are no bacon and eggs in reality, we are going to receive neuronic impacts.

Unless, of course, we find a way to stop thinking about the bacon and eggs. We could think about our hot and heavy date the night before, but that might produce different pictures and neuronic impacts with an altogether different effect, one that would be more trouble than making the bacon and eggs, so we suppress our hot vision, giving our hunger pains a chance to reemerge and the bacon and eggs pop back into our minds, producing more neuronic impacts.

Neither set of neuronic impacts might be sufficient to produce the will to actually hold a picture of reality in recall that doesn't exist in reality, producing the energy it will take to start the process of sending specific electric flows to the specific body parts that would get us moving.

Our hunger is still not strong enough to cause us to form a picture of ourselves getting out of bed.

But the longer we delay, the more insistent the hunger pangs become, the more solid the picture of the bacon and eggs becomes and the less trouble it seems to take to form the pictures necessary to get us out of bed. We begin to combine the random electrical flows we are generating with those producing the hunger pangs and this gives us the energy to get up and go.

When the messages are coming from our subsystems, when our recall is being generated by the current flows that arise from the physical needs of our subsystems to conduct the business they evolved to perform, then our free will is interdicted by necessity.

However, the acts we have committed and continue to commit, the extent to which we have violated and continue to violate societal prohibitions in our pursuit of pleasure also limits our free will.

If we picture an imaginary Will Freeman traipsing down the trodden path to his Sweetpea's house, we can probe the interaction of our freedom to act with our need to act and the cumulative restrictions on our acts violations of Golden Rule Behavior create.

As Will walks merrily along the well-trodden path, his serial recall forms a picture of his journey from the memory units he has stored from previous trips, and he has plenty of time to produce alternate pictures in his recall of what he is going to do with his little Sweetpea after a sumptuous repast. Unbeknownst to Will, however, a rock slide has washed out the path and before his mind is able to form a picture of the changed circumstances in physical reality, pictures which would have produced the neuronic impacts that could have stopped him in his tracks, his foot is already off the edge of the precipice. As his picture of flying bed sheets is replaced with a picture of his own flying limbs trying to gain purchase in physical reality, he is able to grab a branch as he tumbles over, upending himself on a narrow ledge perhaps two body lengths from safety on the other side of the path which is now across the precipice.

Will can't go back up, it is too far, so he forms a picture of his external "I" jumping the chasm. Serial recall shows his external "I" falling short of the other side, and the conflict that results from the picture of his external "I" dropping endlessly down into the chasm against the reality of his intellectual "I" moving his external "I" safely through physical reality stops his mind, which loses track of his body parts, resulting in weak knees, a churning stomach, and a great deal of gas and various noxious liquids traveling in both directions through his body.

Stymied, Will decides to sit down and wait for someone to come down the trail to give him a hand, hoping against hope that that someone isn't his little Sweetpea's husband.

He waits and he waits, and eventually his hunger pangs start to send currents into his mind recalling visions of the sumptuous repast he is missing.

He looks at the chasm and forms a picture of his external "I" making the leap. The neuronic impacts of the leap drown out the hunger pangs and he settles down to wait some more.

Midway through the next day, Will's hunger pangs return in force, and he once again forms a picture of his external "I" making the leap. The resulting neuronic impacts produced by his recall of falling to his death are still strong, and they still overpower his hunger pangs, which means that the fear of jumping blots out the picture of the roast beef dinner, but the hunger pangs are beginning to increase, to come close to equaling the neuronic impacts produced by the picture he recalls of his external "I" jumping the chasm.

Will, of course, has no hope of jumping the chasm if he can't form a picture of himself successfully doing so, and he can't form a picture of himself successfully doing so as long as the neuronic impacts from the pictures leave him weak in the knees.

But his hunger pangs are beginning to overpower the neuronic impacts produced when he tries to form a picture of himself jumping the chasm. Every time he gets the hunger pangs, he recalls the feast, and the worse the hunger pangs get, the more sumptuous the feast becomes and soon the neuronic impacts from the feast are overpowering the neuronic impacts from the jump, which means that the fear of starving blots out the picture of him falling to his death.

Will reaches a point where he no longer has a choice about the jump, he either jumps or he starves. The hunger pangs eventually start to recall a picture of his external "I" lying on the shelf, the meat eaten off his bones by the birds leaving a skeleton of some past glory, producing some really severe neuronic impacts. He starts to grit his teeth and hold the picture of his external "I" jumping in recall regardless of the extent of the neuronic impacts such a picture produces.

He finally make the leap, and either succeeds or ceases to be animated at the bottom of the ravine.

Because ceasing to be animated at the bottom of the ravine would bring our story to an end without delving into how the ubiquitous "I" interacts with our physical needs in the battle of free will with desire, Will's desire invigorated his limbs so that they acted like steel springs, hurling him easily onto the other side of the ravine.

While Will has been stuck on the ledge, however, his Sweetpea has had the time to create second thoughts about the whole affair so that when he arrives, she is all in a tizzy. She had spent the wait putting her external "I" in bed with Will. Because she had spent long hours being subjected to moral instruction dealing with bedding people, and specifically injunctions against bedding people other than her husband, every time she formed a picture of being in bed with Will, her intellectual "I" cycled in the ubiquitous "I". As the picture of her external "I" engaged in sex with Will disagreed with her picture of self maintained by her intellectual "I" as informed by the ubiquitous "I", she suffered severe neuronic impacts as a result.

Until, that is, she started to dwell on Will's strong embrace, his sure touch, his smooth assurances, the feeling of freedom she found with him as the sheets flew hither and yon.

All of a sudden, the neuronic impacts produced by the ubiquitous "I" stopped and desire took over.

Where did the ubiquitous "I" go?

Experiencing no neuronic impacts from recalling her external "I" in bed with Will meant that the picture of her bedding Will now agreed with her intellectual "I", the picture of self that she had in recall.

The intellectual "I" that was forming Sweetpea's pictures of her external "I" was no longer being informed by the ubiquitous "I"!

The intellectual "I" forming in Sweetpea's recall was the intellectual "I" that was created by the pictures she formed during sexual activity. It is the viewpoint contained in the recall she has stored during the times she was engaging in sexual activities.

Our sexual intellectual "I"s are separate and distinct from our intellectual "I"s that are not involved in sexual activities because the level of electrical current at which the recall that makes up our sexual intellectual "I"s is stored is different from the level of current at which our other intellectual "I"s are stored. During sexual activity, our body's subsystems are sending a whole lot of electrical currents into our minds which are totally consonant with the pictures our minds are forming, which are in fact the very pictures with which the electrical currents are associated.

This means that the current level at which the recall of sexual activity is stored is far in excess of the current level at which our minds normally operate and the only way we can recall those pictures is if we can work our bodies up into delivering a sufficient current level for our minds to access the recall.

This is what sexual stimulation is all about. The object of arousal is just that, to get the current level our bodies send to our minds up to the level necessary to get our sexual intellectual "I"s into recall so that our subsystems and our recall are all operating on the same frequency.

Literally!

As soon as Sweetpea has her sexual intellectual "I" in recall, the picture of her external "I" in bed with Will agrees with her sexual intellectual "I".

However, Will's absence puts a fly in her lubricant.

Because of the pressing nature of the instructions her mind is now sending into her subsystems, she is being driven to put her body into a position that matches the recall she is forming of her external "I", and, as she looks around in reality to make the picture of her recall match reality, there is no Will to jump.

This creates even greater neuronic impacts which knocks her sexual intellectual "I" out of recall and allows her non-sexual intellectual "I" along with the ubiquitous "I" realize that with Will missing, there will be no activity to agree with her sexual intellectual "I".

The neuronic impacts of unsatisfied sexual desire are now interpreted as anxiety at Will's absence and concern for his well-being.

But the return of her non-sexual intellectual "I" is informed by the behavioral restraints of the ubiquitous "I" and she now finds herself concerned for an absence with which the ubiquitous "I" informs her intellectual "I" she should totally agree.

So now she gets neuronic impacts from missed sexual satisfaction, anxiety at Will's absence, concern for his safety and a societal disagreement that says she should not even be involved with any of this business to begin with.

To get out of the pain of the neuronic impacts, Will's Sweetpea starts to form pictures of exactly what she is going to do with Will when he arrives, hitting him aside the head with a frying pan or having her husband kill him so she won't have to worry about him ever again.

Occupying her recall with thoughts of mayhem provides her with relief from the neuronic impacts. Unfortunately, forming pictures of her external "I" interacting with Will, even if only through the medium of a frying pan, eventually leads her to form pictures of her external "I" interacting with Will physically, and serial recall starts her dwelling on his strong embrace, his sure touch, his smooth assurances, the feeling of freedom she finds with him as the sheets fly hither and yon, starting the whole process anew.

So it is eminently understandable why Will's Sweetpea is perplexed and full of love and threats when Will finally arrives. Will is famished, but so is she, so he decides to let his Sweetpea slake her thirst before he fills his stomach.

Afterward, as his Sweetpea puts the repast on the table, but before Will makes short work of the first bottle of wine, he finds he has his own little problem with neuronic impacts. Sitting watching his Sweetpea move around the kitchen recalls that she is indeed podded, a married woman, and Will's intellectual "I" also receives a visit from the ubiquitous "I".

Will and his Sweetpea both know they are doing something society has programmed them against doing, and the ubiquitous "I" that embodies society's prohibitions produces the intended result, neuronic impacts.

So as Will and his Sweetpea sit down to dinner, they are both feeling guilty as hell!

Sweetpea has the same problem she had while waiting for Will, only intensified by Will's availability. Will, on the other hand, is overcome by passion every time he concentrates on the rise of her bosom, the shape of her waist, the lushness of her tush, the promise of her legs. His ubiquitous "I" departs and he makes reality his will. Then reality becomes the master as his intellectual "I" returns with the ubiquitous "I" peeking out every time he recalls what he has done, and to make matters worse, because of Sweetpea's threats, he has recurring pictures of himself in a pool of blood at the feet of Sweetpea's husband.

And if that isn't burden enough, his picture of Sweetpea, precious and sweet, an angel among the clouds, is being periodically put into conflict as she becomes hysterical over his lateness, their affair, the possibility of her husband's finding out about the affair and the picture of herself prostrate before an irate society.

Will finally proposes killing Sweetpea's husband and the thought brightens their outlook considerably by focusing their recall on the death of the cause of their pain, her husband. There wouldn't, after all, be any pain if there weren't any husband, right? So focusing on the husband lying in a pool of blood provides temporary surcease from their mutual neuronic impacts by producing recall that does not permit the pictures giving rise to the neuronic impacts to form.

But then the picture of committing murder recalls the punishment for murder and they picture themselves being handcuffed at the police station facing death, or worse, facing being separated from each other, and the neuronic impacts rain down from a different direction, fear.

Sweetpea puts a towel under the door, snuffs the pilot light and turns the gas oven up full under the very correct assumption that the pain, the neuronic impacts, will stop when death stops the electrical flows that produce them. Facing death, however, creates still another set of neuronic impacts, the worst yet, the fear of the unknown, the possibility of retribution by their maker, so they fall into each other's arms, comfort each other, and get relief from the very act that is causing all the trouble.

If the errant couple had conformed to societal dictates, they would have retained their free will because societal prohibitions, while being a limitation on our exercise of free will, do not themselves produce neuronic impacts.

It is the violation of societal dictates that produce neuronic impacts, pain, which in turn limits our free will, sometimes to the point of extinction, when the only relief is to engage in the acts causing the pain.

After all, the ubiquitous "I" is a societal solution to an evolutionary problem!

It 's not perfect.

The ultimate free will, of course, would be to escape being programmed by the ubiquitous "I", to have no societal limitation on our actions.

But, because the mind operates to compare recall with reality, and that comparison produces meaning, to have no standard against which to measure our actions, to have no ubiquitous "I", would be to have no meaning in our lives.

7. EXALTED EMPATHY

Because the ubiquitous "I" isn't in recall and therefore doesn't exist when the sexual acts society seeks to prohibit occur, we might get the idea that society fails in its attempt to program an effective prohibition into our intellectual "I"s and thus causes us considerable harm by programming our normal intellectual "I"s to produce unnecessary neuronic impacts in the form of guilt.

After all, for it to effectively program us against undesirable sexual behavior so that the ubiquitous "I" would be present when our sexual intellectual "I"s are in recall, society would have to program us against sex while we were having sex, defeating the whole purpose of the prohibition.

But we have to remember that we are dealing with a mechanism that evolved to allow us to move safely through physical reality, not to form into social groups.

When we realize that the use of neuronic impacts to program against violations of Golden Rule Behavior is merely a strategy that evolved as a by-product of our ability to create reality in recall when reality is not present in order that we may come together in societies, we can understand why we continue to experience pain, why the societal solution is not perfect.

When a society is using its recall to provide food, shelter and safety, its wealth is communal consisting of the necessities needed for survival. Prosperity, however, creates divisions within the society. These societal divisions, styled in rough percentages as the societal division of ninety, nine and one emerge as we explore how technological proficiency and the prosperity it produces evolves the ubiquitous "I" from one programmed with Golden Rule Behavior to one programmed with Exalted Empathy, a societal dictate that informs us of our overriding concern for those less fortunate than ourselves.

The strategy of using our ability to recall a reality that does not exist in order to connect that recall to punishments in reality which produce neuronic impacts if we attempt to recall actions that would violate societal standards probably only works in a Pavlovian way on ninety-nine percent of society, but ninety-nine percent is apparently a sufficient percentage to allow society to exist, to allow its members to interact without tearing the society apart.

We are driven together for physical reasons, food, shelter and safety, and to escape the pain of the neuronic impacts we receive from viewing the vast canopy of stars for which we have no recall, and if society ceases to provide food, shelter, safety and the gods that provide the answers for the unanswerable, we will drift away and face the night alone.

Society's inability to instill its dictates in one hundred percent of its members and the imperfect instillation of its dictates in the ninety-nine percent is illustrated by society's inability to do anything to alleviate the suffering of its membe.s who, informed by Golden Rule Behavior, have been forced to engage in acts that violate that behavior.

When we have engaged in acts that violate Golden Rule Behavior and our intellectual "I"s have been programmed by a ubiquitous "I" informed by Golden Rule Behavior, we will receive the same neuronic impacts whether we voluntarily engaged in the acts or whether we are forced to engage in the acts.

Neuronic impacts cause real pain and it is a pain for which aspirin provides no relief.

The only way to stop the pain of neuronic impacts is to stop the conflict that is causing the pain and when our acts have left tracks in reality, then the recall is not recall of a reality that doesn't exist in reality, it is recall of a reality that actually occurred in reality, and exists as a fact in our recall.

In *The Model Mind* I used the example of a rape victim to describe the conundrum that results. A rape victim has the ubiquitous "I" in place. She has been forced to commit acts that violate the ubiquitous "I", leaving forevermore in her recall pictures of her external "I" engaged in acts that first cause the ubiquitous "I" to come into recall, and next cause neuronic impacts when the picture of her external "I" engaging in the acts disagrees with the moral imperatives of the ubiquitous "I".

A welcome lover's touch evoking her sexual intellectual "I" recalls the rapists touch, and with it, the recall of her violation of Golden Rule Behavior. This recall in turn eliminates her sexual intellectual "I", allowing her intellectual "I" informed by the ubiquitous "I" to return to recall, effectively destroying any attempt to form a picture of her external "I" engaging in the desired sexual activity, and any ability to act, to engage in sex, at least actively. Her lover, on the other hand, recalls her in the rapist's embrace and ceases to be her lover.

Society can only program the ubiquitous "I", it can not deal with the effects of involuntary violations of societal prohibitions. As long as society's programming is sufficiently effective to keep it from dissolving, society does not concern itself with the rapist that escaped programming nor with the effect on the victims who are left with a lifetime conflict that is not of their own making, other than punishing the offender as an example to instill prohibitions of Golden Rule Behavior in its members.

Society has no interest in victims because helping victims does not program against violations of Golden Rule Behavior!

The rape victim has been crippled because she has been forced to obtain recall of herself violating Golden Rule Behavior, recall which is a continuing source of neuronic impacts, pain.

She has only three choices that will allow her to escape the neuronic impacts.

Because she is already violating societal rules in her recall, she might be driven to violate them in reality, engaging in the acts that agree with her recall to relieve herself, if only momentarily, from the pain the conflict produces.

She can become promiscuous.

Or she can destroy the recall by drugs. Alcohol fuzzes the clear lines of the pictures the mind forms and more importantly allows the recall of nonessential elements to fill holes in the pictures. By giving recall more choices to form pictures that can agree with reality, drinking allows larger and larger variances between reality and recall without the concomitant neuronic impacts.

Or she can kill herself!

While a rape victim is a recurring example of society's inability to produce a perfect solution to the pain societal interactions give rise to, the division of ninety, nine and one is an example of society's attempt to organize itself in a manner that minimizes the remaining neuronic impacts

"Ninety, nine and one" is a catch phrase dealing with a societal division that evolves as a result of the position of intellectual "I"s with respect to society. Just as the position of those around us make them a part of our recall, place them close to our self in recall in what can be described as one of a number of concentric circles surrounding our viewpoint of self, so does the positioning of individuals around the source of a society's wealth produce what has traditionally been viewed as classes but are more accurately classified as levels of awareness.

The division of society into ninety, nine and one deals with the awareness of the members of society concerning the nature of the programming of the ubiquitous "I", and the division arises because, by the very nature of society, certain members of society are positioned to further society's goals and thus are positioned to participate in society's benefits to a greater degree than other members.

On our particular planet there are many societies in competition with one another for resources, and a percentage of the members of any society, the nine percent of the ninety, nine and one, the politicians, the trade lords, the military leaders, the mystical and spiritual paragons and the occult practitioners of empirical science all have to directly violate, participate in direct violations, condone, or at least be aware of the violations of Golden Rule Behavior that are necessary to hold the society together. These violations are necessary to protect the resources the society provides its members, the food, clothing and safety at the basis of the society's existence, or to obtain those resources for its members from other societies when the number and wants of its members outstrip available resources.

A general who, on behalf of the society of which he is a member, orders an enemy city destroyed is no less subject to the consequences of engaging in acts that violate the dictates of the ubiquitous "I", a lifetime of neuronic impacts, of pain, than the rape victim, except the general in deference to his self-sacrifice is given a medal and accorded respect to distract his recall from the acts that would give rise to his pain.

The nine percent of society who are responsible for holding society together by ensuring that the basic purpose of the society, providing for the wants of its members, is satisfied, pay the price because many of their acts violate the morality that is the glue that holds the society together. Because they are the people that hold the society together, they are the best educated and the best provisioned, and that may be what their payment purchases, but they pay the price nonetheless.

The "one" in the division of ninety, nine and one are the one percent of society who escape programming altogether, the one percent whose intellectual "I"s are not informed by the ubiquitous "I" that carries societal dictates into the realm of recall.

The one percent can exercise their free will to engage in acts that society prohibits and receive no adverse physical effects, are not subject to the neuronic impacts that would limit the behavior of and even cause insanity in the other ninety-nine percent and are therefore the psychopaths.

It might at first glance appear that the one percent are inimical to society's interests, that society has an interest in attacking and eliminating psychopaths.

In a perfect world, the one percent might not exist.

However, in the world that we occupy, a world in which societies compete for resources, the one percent are not only very useful, they are absolutely necessary!

Politicians and generals programmed with Golden Rule Behavior may well go down in the face of the pain caused by ordering behavior that violates the basic morality of society. Better a leader with no morals to defend against the barbarians at the gate than a moral leader who might open the gates as an act of compassion or compromise.

When a society's resources are threatened, the services of psychopaths become paramount!

When the reverse occurs, when a society becomes prosperous, when the one percent have destroyed the enemy, stolen its resources and built the fortresses that will protect the society, when the one percent have saved the society, and the society has become prosperous, their utility is nil.

To borrow an empirical favorite, the need for the services of the one percent is inversely proportional to the threat to a society's wealth and well-being. There is no need for their services whatsoever in a prosperous society, but their services rule absolutely when society's resources, its prosperity, is threatened.

The ninety percent, of course, are the rest of us who, exchanging our labor and our agreement to conform to societal dictates in exchange for the food, shelter, safety and the beliefs society provides, remain unaware of the sacrifices of the nine and the one, self-sacrifice on the part of the former and just sacrifice on the part of the latter.

Trade satisfies society's social contract to provide food, shelter and safety to its members. Nowhere do we find a clearer statement of the organization of wealth around trade than in the globally oriented society that has grown up as the United States. Trade benefits all members of a society by providing the means for all members to obtain the food, shelter and safety that would otherwise have to obtained on an individual basis. In return, the members of society agree to engage in appropriate behavior, which includes providing the labor society needs to carry out its obligations.

Identifying ninety percent of a particular society as being unaware of the basic fact of existence that underlies any society on this particular planet, that our food, shelter and safety come at the expense of others, is a fearful thing to do, but we can not analyze how the mind generates behavior if we don't face the simple facts of our existence.

If ninety percent of society were aware that to hold the society together with Golden Rule Behavior requires continual violations of that Golden Rule Behavior, there would be no society!

Leaving the violations of Golden Rule Behavior to the nine percent that are not particularly affected by the violations, and occasionally to the one percent that feel no pain at all, and allowing the nine percent a greater participation in the benefits of society, better food and shelter, in exchange for the ninety percent being allowed to remain ignorant of the violations of Golden Rule Behavior required for a society to exist is at the basis of the societal contract.

The ninety percent do not want the neuronic impacts awareness produces, they want the food, shelter and safety that eliminates the neuronic impacts that, without the societal contract, would result from having to provide for themselves, do the taking themselves on a daily basis.

It might be more complimentary to refer to the ninety percent as peasants or the masses, the proletariat, the common man or the great unwashed as is traditional, rather than to denigrate them by implying that they are unaware, but the simple fact is, we enter the social contract, we agree to conform our behavior to minimize our neuronic impacts and we simply don't care to exercise the level of awareness that would bring us neuronic impacts from a different source.

Just as the foot soldiers do not need to share the recall of the general deploying the troops, the vast majority of those that contract with society, who agree to refrain from acting in violation of societal prohibitions in exchange for food, shelter and safety for their young do not need to share the recall of those they deputize with the authority to ensure that the contract is carried out.

In fact, an aware foot soldier is an asset to the enemy!

The purpose of deputizing a small percentage of society with the authority to ensure that the contract is carried out is to relieve the vast majority of the members of society of the neuronic impacts that carrying out the contract involves.

We march out to steal the farm land of others to the tune of God and Country because we don't want to know that we are marching out to ensure food for ourselves and our young, but somebody has to know and thus suffer the neuronic impacts for the rest of us.

The nine percent are aware to a certain extent that to preserve society, to deliver the contract, requires acts that violate societal prohibitions. These people live within a society and are taught to honor the prohibitions that define Golden Rule Behavior, but because they have been educated or have risen through the ranks to fill jobs which have to deal with reality, with preserving society and ensuring that society meets its contractual obligations to it members, they have to deal with violations of Golden Rule Behavior, or have to order others to violate Golden Rule Behavior, or have to violate Golden Rule Behavior themselves. The position is analogous to the layers of management that occupy the uneasy buffer between policy makers and workers. People that occupy these positions have to wear two hats, one, to understand and carry out policy, the other to persuade workers to conform their work to that policy.

With two hats, the nine percent are in perpetual conflict with themselves and with societal dictates, *even if the ubiquitous "I" that informs their behavior is not the same ubiquitous "I" that is informed by Golden Rule Behavior!*

Just as we as individuals have common recall among those in our inner concentric circles of recall, so too does the nine percent, isolated by their awareness, have common recall that differs from the recall informed by Golden Rule Behavior.

Because our minds work by comparison, we compare recall and reality, and because our minds generate our intellectual "I"s which in turn generate our external "I"s, our intellectual "I"s are formed by watching our external "I"s interact with others in external reality. The sum total of these interactions produces the prohibitions that define Golden Rule Behavior and produces the ubiquitous "I". Although we come together in society to satisfy common physical needs, those we associate with in the society are determined by a commonality of our recall. And as prosperity evolves society, society moves from defining prohibited behavior, from prohibiting acts, to requiring acts, demanding the positive performance of active conduct.

Purveyors of the hunting and gathering myth, that society comes together as the result of a shared interest in survival, that individuals form into hunting parties that can go out and overpower the beast, do not take into consideration the neuronic impacts that drive us together. We are driven to seek out those that are like us because when we are with others who are not like us, we cannot see our external "I"s in those around us. We don't know from nothing when we start out, and very rarely do we know much when we end up, but what we do know we get from looking at those around us.

We shape our intellectual "I"s by looking at how others like us in external reality act, creating recall that shows our external "I"s acting in a similar fashion, and then acting in external reality in accordance with that recall. We don't fashion our external "I"s after dogs or cats or cows, we fashion our external "I"s after others in external reality who appear the same as our external "I"s appear or appear as we want to appear.

Once we have stored a sufficient number of pictures in recall to generate our intellectual "I"s, we tend to associate with others to the extent they are present in the recall that produces our intellectual "I"s. We are forming and storing pictures that include a picture of ourselves at the rate of fifty or sixty pictures a second. If we spend our time with our family, then the members of our family will be stored with the recall that generates our intellectual "I"s.

Our physical reaction to individuals who occupy large portions of our recall along with our intellectual "I"s is similar to our physical reaction when we have recall for the objects we see in reality.

When we have recall for what we see in reality, we have no neuronic impacts and we feel comfortable.

When we are around others, those others fill our recall in a manner similar to our intellectual "I"s, with the more recall we have of others, the more those others agree with our recall. We feel comfortable with people that are already in our recall because those people agree with our recall.

If we don't have someone in recall, then we feel uncomfortable with that person because we are dealing with something in reality for which we as yet have no recall and we respond to the resulting neuronic impacts.

Our neighbors occupy less of our recall than our family while our fellow worshipers may occupy more of our recall than our neighbors. If we live in a town, then the people that make up the town occupy our recall to one extent or another, together with the people we go to school with and the people we work with.

The position of those in our concentric circles of recall is similar to the position of those who would drive us to take revenge for their loss in our recall.

We break down others in our recall in accordance to sex, national origin and race, even religion, many times region, always generation, perhaps by location, people from the wrong side of the tracks, or those on the right side of the tracks, the people that belong to the country club.

Just as the death of a person in external reality can create neuronic impacts by recalling what no longer exists in reality, so too do the people that populate our recall drive us to spend time with them over others. We are driven by neuronic impacts away from that which is not familiar because it is not in recall and toward that which is in recall, to that which is familiar.

The mind's basic operation to match recall and reality to avoid the pain of neuronic impacts drives us into groups made up of members who have shared recall. Because we form our intellectual "I"s by reference to the interaction of our external "I"s with others in physical reality, the answers we produce to explain reality where there can be no recall, where we came from, what we are, how reality works, as well as how much of reality is included in the area for which there can be no recall, are consensus answers. Because we live in a society that defines both our moral behavior and the answers to questions that are not apparent in reality, society provides the answers, and the answers society provides are the consensus reality of that society.

To go against consensus reality is difficult because consensus reality does not reside in our external "I"s, but rather in our intellectual "I"s for answers dealing with physical reality, and in the ubiquitous "I" for answers dealing with morality.

We can't disagree with recall that is part of our self.

The operation of our minds to avoid conflicts, the pain of neuronic impacts, drives us to cling to likes. In times of trouble, we don't seek out people that are not in our recall. We seek out people in our recall. Just as we surround our external "I"s with a space that cannot be encroached upon by others without causing us neuronic impacts, we have comfort zones that extend to our social interactions with others.

Thus, our intellectual "I"s occupy the center of a series of concentric circles, with the smallest circle comprised of the people that occupy our recall the most, and the outermost circle comprised of the distant barbarians about whom we know nothing factual but of whom we have a picture painted by the consensus, a picture which, for us, is reality because, having no reality to contradict the pictures that have been painted for us, the picture is all we have in our recall.

If we are prosperous, if society is prosperous, then we can venture out beyond the little circles that make up our primary comfort zones into wider circles without fear of endangering our external "I"s.

As long as we are fed and sheltered against the elements, and safe, our concerns expand beyond our individual inner concentric circles.

We can throw our external "I"s into foreign company.

However, when times get tough we shrink back into our recall. When we are forced to choose, we will help a member of our own country before we help a member of another country, we will help a member of our race before we help a member of another race, we will help a member of our town or school before we help a member of another town or school, and we will above all help a member of our family before we help a member of another family.

To do otherwise is to be altruistic, and while the more prosperous a society is, the more it values altruism, altruism does not put food on the table.

Altruism removes food from the table!

We have free will, and we can choose to be selfish or selfless. But the extent to which we can be selfless is in direct proportion to how much food we have on our own table. The basic morality of society is created by the need for its members to come together to produce food. When society becomes prosperous, when it begins to produce an excess of food, the need for the prohibitions that define morality diminish.

The ubiquitous "I" that prosperity evolves is not as interested in prohibiting acts that it considers selfish as it is in requiring acts to further its selfless goals.

Prohibitions against licentiousness give way to the altruistic imperative that we must help others less fortunate than ourselves!

How does a society become prosperous?

Prosperity is the product of technology which in turn is the product of engineering.

Engineering creates the dividing line between recall that reflects reality and recall that reflects blithering idiocy, occult bullcrap about how things would be if an ideal universe were contained in a boundless empirical mind.

Engineering takes the measure of the world and then tests those measurements, creating, as a result, changes in physical reality that accommodate our continued existence.

Empirical science mimics this process to fool itself and society into believing that its theoretical musings about the nature of reality and how reality operates, musings manufactured totally in recall and untestable in reality, are actually reality. Empirical science claims that mathematically predicting facts which are not known at the time of the prediction, or at least not known to be connected to the mathematical prediction at the time of the prediction, prove the concepts predicting the facts to also be facts. Thus, by deluding itself into believing that the straight-line attraction of gravity predicts the circular motion of the planets, it believes that gravity is a property of mass, a bald assumption. It then goes on to plug the bald assumption it now believes to be a real fact into all sorts of mathematical silliness to come up with black holes in space, dark matter between the stars and matter formation in the center of stars.

Empirical science then turns around and claims credit for engineering accomplishments while sneering at the engineers making those accomplishments, labeling them mere engineers and their accomplishment mere engineering, nowhere near as exciting and godly as scientifically determining how much light could peek over the event horizon of a black hole if a black hole could allow light to peek over its event horizon.

On the other hand, using our mind to move us through physical reality rather than to make up a recall without reference to physical reality results in neuronic impacts when we bump into things.

Being opposed by physical reality produces purple flimgasts, things for which we have no recall. The failure of our recall to produce pictures that match reality produces neuronic impacts which force our minds to alter their current level in an attempt to come up with a picture that does match the picture we are receiving from reality. When something invisible in physical reality restrains our movement, restricts our freedom of choice as to which way we wish to move, we alter the current level running through our minds as a result of the neuronic impacts and their electrical feedback until we can form a picture of physical reality that will allow us to once again move through physical reality.

If our path is blocked by a fallen tree, then we form a picture of the path without the tree and test alternate pictures of our external "I"s taking action in physical reality to create a path without a tree blocking it.

The same process, altering current levels to change the elements of physical reality and then using the neuronic impacts when the resulting recall doesn't match reality to create a reality that matches recall, drives us to clear the path in front of us, drives us to turn the tree into a roof over our heads to keep the rain out, drives us to perfect tools to fashion implements to obtain and prepare our food, and drives us to create light in the houses we build to dispel the darkness the walls of those houses produce.

The production of technology is the result of the mind's ability to hold pictures in recall that do not exist in reality, and then to change the pictures in recall by changing the current level of the individual elements of the picture so that other elements are recalled.

This is creativity.

Once we have a picture of recall that doesn't exist in reality stored in memory, then when we recall that picture, the failure of the picture to match reality produces neuronic impacts that drive us to alter reality to conform it to our recall.

This is not rocket science!

Rocket science is thinking that our made up pictures of reality actually reflect that reality. If we think that mass is a property of matter, installed in that matter by our god when the universe was formed, then we will never, ever form a picture in our recall of ourselves attempting to overcome this most universal of obstacles in reality, the obstacle that holds us to the surface of the Earth. If we are so arrogant as to believe that we know why objects fall, we will never, ever attempt to figure out why those objects actually fall and we will never, ever attempt to form the pictures necessary to create the technology that will allow us to eliminate that force. We will instead build airplanes with wings that swim through the atmosphere like fish swim through water, or rockets that push against the atmosphere like squid push against water, filling our recall with all sorts of problem solving that obscures the basic questions presented by reality, questions dealing with motion and force.

The problem with not clearly defining the line between those things for which recall can never exist other than by naming, the god we chose to be responsible for the existence of matter in nothing, and those things for which we can produce recall is that when we put too many items on the side of our god, we place them outside the realm of our engineers. It is not the engineer's fault that he builds wings and jet engines because the empirical science that has perverted his procedures has arrogated the answers to questions about physical reality as occult, belonging to God, and then made those answers incapable of being recalled as other than words, the force that makes objects fall mass/gravity, the force that makes the planet rotate angular momentum, the structure of light a wave and therefore nonexistent, the effect of electricity a moving charge, the movement of a magnet the result of molecular magnets, the nothing of space something that can be warped, the measurement of time flexible.

The extent to which we allow nonanswers to restrict our ability to alter recall to produce pictures of reality that do not exist in reality defines our limitation in physical reality because it is our ability to engineer changes in physical reality that allows us to accommodate physical reality to our existence. Because we evolved in the physical reality in which we find ourselves, our continued existence is dependent on that physical reality. If there are substantial changes in that physical reality, the Earth becomes cold, its atmosphere drifts away, or it just simply blows up, then our existence will cease.

Thus, our ability to change the physical reality in which we exist, the success we achieve in engineering our environment to accommodate our existence will determine the extent to which we can extend our range of survivability because survivability depends on our being independent of the environment in which we evolved.

The ability of our minds to extend our range of survivability in physical reality is a by-product of the mechanism that evolved simply to move us through physical reality. The necessity of having a physical structure that could record the difference between reality and a picture of that reality formed from recall became, once pictures of recall could be held in that structure regardless of the neuronic impacts produced when recall didn't agree with reality, an entirely new evolutionary characteristic, one that could be used to make us independent of our environment.

Once our minds became a marvelous tool capable of changing the universe, then so long as the unseen presences guiding the mind, the gods the mind ascribed to, weren't empowered to limit the mind's ability to form in recall pictures of the possible, that tool could be used to replace our labor and produce prosperity.

However, when we abdicate our possibilities to rules and laws laid down by the force that made our matter, when we leave questions dealing with physical reality entangled with the question of existence for which we can have no recall, then we have abdicated our minds, and our future to what we have made up and put in our recall.

To the extent that we allow reality to inform our recall, however, we can use this tool, our mind, to create a technology that produces more than we need to exist in that reality.

We use our minds to produce the technology that results in the prosperity that alters the ubiquitous "I" that controls our actions.

We allocate what we don't need outward in the same series of concentric circles into which we retreat when we select who we will stand with against the world. We take care of those closest to ourselves first, those that appear the most in our recall along with our intellectual "I"s, first family, then friends and neighbors, coreligionists, fellow citizens of town, state and country. After we have enough to feed and shelter ourselves and our families, we have an excess which can be made available to others who through age, physical condition, or position are not capable of producing food and shelter for themselves.

The prosperity of a society dictates how much work that society has to put into producing food and shelter. The more prosperous a society is, the less work it has to invest in producing food and shelter. The less work that goes into producing food and shelter, the more recall there is available for creativity, for producing recall that doesn't exist in reality, and thus for engineering technology.

Technology, in turn, reduces the amount of work necessary to produce food and shelter and thus increases prosperity.

When our environment produces subsistence only in response to the work of all available hands, our hands are being directed by a recall busy with forming pictures of our external "I"s moving our hands in physical reality. If we are spending all of our time recalling pictures of our external "I"s hoeing the row in physical reality, we have no time to use our recall to form pictures that don't exist in reality.

In situations where every calorie of work goes into survival, the only way society can survive is to follow Golden Rule Behavior. We would have little patience for the sexual dalliances whose only result would lead to a diminution of the available food and shelter and even less use for the thief who takes our food or the murderer who eliminates a worker.

But with prosperity, more recall is freed up to contemplate reality and create possible changes to that reality and the resulting technology leverages labor to increase the available food and shelter freeing up still more recall.

The resulting prosperity begins to produce a class of people close to the source of wealth that become the nine percent who do not have to work to produce food and shelter, and whose recall is therefore free to create recall of realities that do not exist. Creating technology requires mental effort, while creating variations on ways to satisfy the need for food and shelter merely requires prosperity. With more recall available, and with idyll minds the devil's playground, all sorts of variations concerning what external "I"s can and might be doing in physical reality become the source of contemplation.

Because morality exists, it is a reality, and because it is a reality that has been assigned to society's god, it is a reality for which there is no recall. Just as explanations for physical reality are consensus conclusions as to how that reality operates, so too is morality a consensus conclusion as to how people in society should behave.

Morality is inherent in society so long as bare survival is its only goal. When prosperity frees up recall to form pictures of external "I"s engaged in activities that aren't necessary for bare survival, and work is not necessary, then not engaging in the acts dreamed up in recall will result in neuronic impacts. As society finds that acts that violate Golden Rule Behavior do not immediately detract from its basic contractual obligation to provide food and shelter, then the programming of the ubiquitous "I" begins to treat the prohibitions that define Golden Rule Behavior differently.

The people engaged in the violations, after all, are the same people that define the behavior and do the programming. These people are clustered around the wealth that is being produced by society and, because they look to each other for how to behave, create a consensus apart from the society as a whole where actions are still restrained by the standards of Golden Rule Behavior.

Two things begin to occur as prosperity takes over the recall of the nine percent of society that is centered around the production of wealth.

First, because their intellectual "I"s are capable of visualizing all sorts of acts their external "I"s can engage in, and their intellectual "I"s are continually testing those acts against the neuronic impacts they produce when their external "I"s are visualized performing those acts, and their external "I"s then go out and engage in the acts, prosperity brings tremendous personal freedom of choice. With society loosening up both its legal prohibitions against acts and its programming of the ubiquitous "I" against engaging in acts, the consequences of engaging in all sorts of acts, both legal, the fear of loss of freedom and body parts, and psychological, the neuronic impacts interpreted as guilt when societal prohibitions are violated, become minimal and the freedom to act expands.

Second, empathy produces neuronic impacts perceived as guilt when the newly endowed nine percent view others in physical reality without the same freedoms.

Our intellectual "I"s are the sum total of all of the pictures of our external "I"s formed and stored in recall. As the external "I"s of the nine percent enjoy personal freedom to exercise free will and freedom from expending work to produce food and shelter for themselves, their intellectual "I"s begin to include concepts of freedom from want and freedom of choice to act that become inherent in their concept of self.

When the nine percent move through external reality and see others in external reality that do not have the freedoms inherent in their intellectual "I"s, empathy asserts itself and the effect is similar to seeing their external "I"s in reality lying in a pool of blood, dead.

Their intellectual "I"s create a picture of their external "I"s in the plight of others without the same freedom, without the same choices, without the same prosperity, and they experience neuronic impacts.

When the nine percent see those less fortunate, they are driven to help them because they cannot help but place their external "I"s in the same situation, and when they do so, they receive neuronic impacts which can only be stopped by engaging in acts that are intended to raise the condition of those less fortunate to their own level.

The empathy that produced Golden Rule Behavior, do unto others as you would have them do unto yourself, evolves with prosperity into Exalted Empathy, the requirement that those informed by Exalted Empathy raise those less fortunate than themselves to their own level of prosperity no matter what the cost.

8. THE FAILURE TO PRODUCE ACCURATE TECHNOLOGY

Technology is the source of prosperity in society. Prosperity provides us with safety, mobility, awareness, recreation and pleasure but it also provides us with the time to perfect our picture of physical reality so that we can extend our range of survivability in physical reality.

If we base our technology on a delusional picture of physical reality, then instead of using the ability of our minds to create technology that will extend our range of survivability into the universe, we will use our minds to create technology that will attempt to preserve our short lived pleasures.

The mind is a detector that evolved to move us safely through physical reality. It is a physical mechanism that evolved a system of exception to alert us when something in physical reality is different from what we have experienced and therefore might be unsafe.

The mind operates by forming pictures. It receives information about external reality from the senses, primarily through the eyes. This information, in the form of electrical flows, disbalances the mind, which, without the electrical flows, is an electrical structure held into a web of stable equilibrium by the charges of the particles that make it up.

When the mind is disbalanced, the disbalance, the movement of the particles that make up the mind out of their positions of stable equilibrium, produces a representation of reality that corresponds to the electrical flows that bounce off the hard edges of physical reality and therefore produces a picture of that physical reality.

It is the comparison process, the match of reality with recall, whether the recall is a picture, a word or a phrase, that provides us with the sense of meaning.

The same electrical flows that form the picture, the representation of reality, travel throughout the wet works of the brain picking up memory units representing reality which are stored in the neurons. These memory units are stored at an electrical charge that represents the sum total of the elements of the picture that they contain. Recall operates by matching the charges of the stored memory units with the charge of the electrical flows that are forming representations of physical reality in the mind.

The transport of memory units to the mind is the process of recall.

As both sets of electrical flows, those from the senses and those encoded in memory units stored in the neurons, stream into our minds, our minds have a recall of the reality through which we are moving, and a recall of our experience having moved through that reality before. If we have moved through the reality before, and done so safely, then as long as reality matches recall, we can do nothing but continue to move through the reality our minds are recalling.

When something appears in reality that disagrees with what we are recalling, our minds stop operating and the electrical flows that have been operating them, having nowhere to go, enter our bodies, disrupting our subsystems so that we have to pause in our movement through physical reality.

We can't move in physical reality if we can't form a picture of ourselves moving in physical reality.

The pause gives our minds time to alter our recall in an attempt to come up with something that matches reality so that we can start to form pictures that would once again allow us to continue moving safely through physical reality.

If we can not come up with recall that matches reality, if we find ourselves in a totally new reality, then we have to stop and puzzle out what is going on, create pictures by analogy, filling in blanks with similar recall before we can continue. If we can not do this, we cannot continue to move through reality because our minds cannot form a picture of us doing so.

Without having recall of the reality in which we are attempting to move, we would have to send out scouts to come up with a safe way to navigate the unknown.

Attention is what occurs when the reality we find ourselves in and our recall of that reality do not agree.

Our minds stop working.

When our minds stop working, our bodies receive neuronic impacts made up of the electrical flows that were operating our minds.

The mind does not start to perform its evolved task until it stops operating!

This is why the mind's operation has remained elusive.

It operates by exception.

It is only when our minds cease to operate that our attention is called to the changes in reality that are causing our minds to stop operating.

When our bodies are disturbed from their normal operation, they notify our minds by sending them electrical signals. If we are inattentive and bump into a brick wall, the brick wall announces itself by disrupting the parts of our body that it comes into contact with, and these body parts send electrical flows into our minds.

In the same manner, unexpected electrical flows that invade our bodies when our minds cease to operate result in return messages, discomfort.

However, because there is no external source of our pain, nothing in physical reality we can point a finger at to blame for our discomfort, we focus our attention on reality rather than on recall.

The returning flows cause memory units to begin reentering our minds, creating random recall in our minds in an attempt to come up with something that agrees with the pictures streaming in from our senses.

When there's something about reality that is not in our recall, it attracts our attention.

When something attracts our attention, we become conscious of it.

"Conscious" is a term that means aware.

Empirical science turned the adverb "conscious" into the noun "consciousness" because it has no idea how the mind operates. As in all areas of physical reality, it produces a word to name that for which it has no recall, the mind, and then claims that the actual operation, the mind, doesn't exist.

When we realize that our recall is made up of serial pictures each of which includes a picture of our self, and which thus creates a point of view that is aware of itself in reality, we can put a face on consciousness. Nothing reaches our consciousness until our attention is called to it, and the only way our attention is called to something is if the mind's normal operation is stopped as a result of a disagreement between recall and reality.

Consciousness is not a mysterious entity that exists as a result of an occult process involving chemical messengers flitting about among neurons which have become connected by happenstance.

Consciousness is an operation, the process of comparing recall and reality!

Meaning results from comparing recall with reality.

When we do not have recall for something, we have no comparison and thus no meaning. It is the process of producing recall that matches reality that produces meaning.

It doesn't matter what the recall is, whether it is pictures, words or phrases, so long as it matches the picture of reality we have in our minds, we have meaning.

Measurements merely ensure that the picture against which we are matching recall represents reality.

The nature of meaning, its source in matching recall with the picture of reality in our mind can be experienced by producing the absence of meaning while the mind is operating. Objects in reality are inanimate matter and thus have no meaning in and of themselves. If we focus on an object in physical reality so that we are recalling precisely what we are seeing, we cease to recall even though the electrical flows are continuing to operate in our brain.

This is because we do not store duplicate memory units we have already stored at a particular charge.

When the mind forms memory units that are carried into the wet works of the brain and those memory units encounter memory units already stored at that particular charge, then the transaction is netted out, with no new memory units stored.

The only recall is the same recall that is already forming in the mind, the precise representation of reality on which we are focusing our attention.

As a child, I used a clock to accomplish this effect. I was not subject to a great deal of environmental noise where I grew up so that when the house was silent, the ticking of a clock became intrusive. When we sit still in a quiet room with only the ticktock of a clock to mark changes in reality, focusing on a single picture, keeping the eyes stationary, actually freezes our mind. Our mind doesn't stop operating because it still recalls the ticking of the clock when sensory input produces the tick of the clock, but for all intents and purposes the mind is frozen with its recall exactly matching reality.

When this occurs, reality ceases to have any meaning because when we are recalling exactly what we are seeing, we are not experiencing the comparison process. The absence of the comparison process allows us to see the object we are focusing on for what it is, an object in reality with no inherent meaning.

The electrical flows that operate our mind are not disturbing our body so that there is no interaction between the two, no instructions to the muscles to move to match the pictures of reality our mind is forming, no neuronic impacts when reality doesn't agree with those pictures as the body adjusts its position in reality, no variation in recall, just the ticktock, ticktock, ticktock of the clock to mark that passage of time and thus the fact of our existence.

This surreal exercise highlights what meaning is by eliminating it!

The simple act of forming pictures of external reality in our mind produces no meaning.

We also experience the absence of meaning in physical objects in a more painful way when there are changes in physical reality that require our attention so that we can continue to move safely through that reality. When we have no recall that compares with the pictures we are receiving from reality, the failure of the comparison process stops our minds from operating and the electrical flows that were operating them move into our bodies, causing us pain..

It is the process of matching recall with the pictures of reality that we form that gives objects meaning and provides us with the absence of neuronic impacts we feel as understanding!

Meaning, understanding, comprehension have always presented problems of definition. Empirical science phrased the problem in terms of the only activity it was capable of performing, putting things in categories and it has long wondered how the mind can categorize things.

Empirical science is incapable of answering its own question, however, because the mind's operation can't be categorized and if something can't be categorized, it doesn't, as far as empirical science is concerned, exist.

We can easily comprehend the mechanical way the mind categorizes things by the process the mind compares recall with reality. The current level the reality generates recalls the memory units stored in the neuronic storage chambers of the brain. As a result, the mind stores things by grouping pictures of the things in accordance with the level of the electrical flows the pictures of those things produce.

The mind stores pictures at current levels and similar pictures are stored at similar current levels.

When we categorize rocks, we look at gray round rocks and store all gray round rocks at a similar current level. When we see gray round rocks, we recall gray round rocks, not black jagged rocks, which we have stored at a different current level.

If we see a black jagged rock, we recall black jagged rocks and we have what we see categorized by what we have recalled, which is everything stored at a similar current level, black jagged rocks.

If we have only these two categories stored in recall, and we run across a black round rock, the black round rock catches our attention because we have no rocks stored at a current level of black round rocks and thus we have no recall for what we see. If we focus on the element of color, we can access black rocks, but we come up with jagged rocks, not round rocks. If we focus on the shape, we come up with gray rocks, but not black rocks.

We shrug our shoulders and create a new category, black round rocks.

We then find that we have new categories. We have one category dealing with shape, round rocks that can be either black or gray and another category dealing with color, black rocks that can be round or jagged.

We have begun to categorize the categories.

The whole process of empirical science is to put everything into categories so that when we see something, we know what it is, it is a pelican or an octopus.

Being able to name things, which is the process of creating recall that matches reality, provides us with meaning for those things.

It is difficult to believe that the nature of meaning is that simple, but it is.

Meaning is the agreement of recall with reality. If we have no recall, we have no meaning, no understanding, no comprehension.

When reality is forthright, when it deals with objects in physical reality, meaning presents no problem. Meaning only becomes a problem when our attention is directed at the motion of objects in reality because there is nothing forthright in reality dealing with the cause of the motion that we can put in recall.

We can make up something and put it in recall so that we think we comprehend what we see and therefore have meaning, but what we make up has no counterpart in physical reality.

Because the source of our existence also has no counterpart in physical reality, we confuse questions of motion with questions of existence even though questions of motion deal with operations in physical reality where accurate meaning and thus precise recall is of the utmost importance, while questions surrounding our existence are questions for which we can have no recall and thus are questions of personal preference.

We will never be able to measure what makes a rock fall because the physical force is too small to put a ruler to. We will never know what makes the planet rotate on its axis for the same reason. We will never really know what light or electricity or magnetism is because what makes them up is too small for us to see and we therefore can not form a picture of them in our minds. We have nothing from reality for which we can produce recall.

What we do have from reality is an object falling, a rotating planet, light that can slow down and, with no apparent force, speed back up, electricity that can produce light and magnetism that can produce electricity.

Empirical science, having only the ability to categorize things to match recall with reality to produce what it defines as meaning and comprehension, places real questions about physical reality, questions dealing with force and motion, questions that need accurate pictures if we are to produce a technology that reflects physical reality, with the things for which we can have no recall.

How we define the things for which we can have no recall will define how accurate our pictures of physical reality are and thus determine how capable we are of producing a technology that can alter physical reality to our benefit. If we don't have a clear picture of the force that is holding us to the surface of the Earth, the technology we produce to move us against that force will have no relation to reality.

If we mistake the things for which we can have no recall with questions of the current operation of physical reality for which we can produce precise descriptions of process, we will confuse questions dealing with physical reality with the provenance of our god, questions concerning our existence.

The concept of our creator, the force that produces matter in nothing, can never be more than a belief.

However, we can produce recall about everything else in physical reality because physical reality exists.

But knowing about reality, its size and dimensions, does not tell us anything about that reality. Knowing that black rocks are black rocks may feel good, but it doesn't tell us anything about how physical reality operates.

And that is exactly what we need to know!

There is a whole range of recall that exists between categorizing rocks and conceptualizing the creator of the rock, and that recall requires a mechanical explanation of process to explain its operation because we are dealing with questions of motion and the force that produces that motion, and these are questions of operation.

Questions of force and motion cannot be answered by the process of categorization, by creating comprehension through the process of comparison.

When empirical science sets out to categorize things that are not forthright in reality and are not in the provenance of our creator, questions of how physical reality operates, it categorizes the movement it measures and leaves the explanation of that movement to our creator.

Empirical science says that objects fall, a measurable fact, then concludes that they fall because matter has a property, gravity, that makes objects fall. When we want to know what gravity is, we find that our creator installed it as a property of matter when he created the matter.

Empirical science says that planets move, a measurable fact, then concludes that they move because our creator put all matter in motion moving in straight lines, installing motion as a property of matter when he created the matter.

When we point out that no matter moves in straight lines and gravity doesn't cause the moon to fall to the surface of the Earth or planets to fall into the sun, empirical science says that our creator installed the precise amount of straight-line motion in matter to keep it from being overcome by the gravity, a precise amount of which our creator installed in the matter to make it overcome the straight-line motion.

What empirical science does for us is to protect us from the neuronic impacts we would receive if we didn't have something to recall when we see an object fall. It simulates comprehension by creating a category, producing a name, calling the force that makes something fall gravity so that we now have recall, the word gravity, that explains why objects fall.

But then, as we form and hold pictures in recall, we should notice another hole in the picture.

We should notice that we don't have a picture of what matter is doing that makes objects fall.

The conflict of recall and reality should get our attention, bring a hole in the picture of falling objects into full consciousness. The picture is incomplete because of the absence of the recall that explains reality. It is this absence that should get our attention.

The missing element of the picture is what generates our question.

Questions are things for which we have no recall, holes in the pictures our minds form and answers are things we put in recall so that we have recall to fill in the holes in our pictures of reality.

We are driven to fill in the holes of our recall because holes produce neuronic impacts, pain.

It is extremely important that we ask the right questions when we are trying to fill in the holes in our pictures of physical reality. If we ask the wrong question, we will fill in the holes of our recall with occult bullcrap and end up with a distorted picture of reality.

If we ask what makes objects fall instead of asking how the force is produced that makes objects fall, how the force moves and how the force acts on matter to make the objects fall, we will be able to come up with any answer we want to make up to explain why objects fall, and that is why empirical science comes up with occult answers that assign questions of force and motion to our creator, concluding that force and motion were installed in the matter by the creator when the matter was created.

Asking the right question is so very important that it deserves to be highlighted by an absurdity, the crown jewel of empirical science, motion in space.

When stargazers look up at the sky and see motion, their attention is drawn to that motion. The cause of the motion is a hole in the picture they form of the heavens.

You and I, and the rest of the unsophisticated minds that are outside the inside would look down at our feet and, finding that it takes force to pick them up off the Earth, ask, what is making the objects we see, the moon and the planets, move.

Sophisticated stargazers, however, know better. They ask the question, what is making the moon and the planets slow down!

If we pursued our question, what is moving the moon and the planets, we might come up with an explanation for the force that is causing the movement.

What do the stargazers come up with?

Things that cannot be detected in the black expanse of space, holes in space as black as space itself and dark matter detectable by no telescope, things that draw our attention away from the fact that they have no answer for the most obvious question of our reality, why the sun comes up every morning.

Failing to ask the proper questions about falling objects is more subtle. If we ask the question what makes things fall instead of how the force that makes things fall is generated, we can answer, they fall because there is something about the Earth toward which they are falling that is attracting them. All we have to do is categorize what that something is and we will have simulated comprehension that explains why objects fall to the Earth.

How do we categorize matter?

We categorize it by size and shape, by its properties, its characteristics.

Empirical science does the same thing with force and motion. It creates a property of matter that attracts other objects.

Thus, when we see something fall, we can say it's a property of the object to fall.

It is a property of attraction.

What else has a property of attraction, empirical science asks.

Magnets.

But magnets attract and repel, the Earth only attracts.

Ah, empirical science sighs, we have two categories which verifies the category of gravity as a property of matter just like color.

We have thus, by using the tried and true process of creating categories, names, created comprehension. We believe we have created a category even though we have only categorized one thing by comparing one category with a different category that has similar characteristics. We compare the Earth's attraction to a magnet's attraction and create a category of attraction. We then distinguish magnets which attract and repel from the Earth which attracts all over.

Empirical science is treating questions of force and motion just like it treats gray round and jagged black rocks!

It doesn't have the foggiest idea what the nature of the force is that is causing the motion in either the falling rock or the magnet, the actual answer we need to know if we are going to create an accurate picture of physical reality upon which we can base our technology, but, what the heck, empirical science says it knows and we aren't going to question the answer because knowing makes us feel good.

We haven't understood anything about what is making objects fall or what makes magnets attract and repel. We don't know how the force that makes objects fall is generated, we don't know how it travels from one place to another, we don't know how it acts on matter to move it, and we don't know what the matter is that is being moved, the structural nature of the matter itself that allows the force to act upon it in the way it does, but we don't have to recall all of this to satisfy ourselves that we understand why an object falls.

It falls because gravity is a property of matter!

What empirical science is doing is categorizing operations instead of objects and naming operations merely simulates comprehension rather than telling us what is actually going on in physical reality.

There are not two types of gravity, there are not two types of planetary rotation, there are not two types of light, there are not two types of electricity and there are not two types of magnets. But, with nothing with which to categorize gravity, and driven to categorize it as something to avoid being subjected to neuronic impacts, pain, we'll just call it a property like color or texture or shape to simulate comprehension.

Light, well, that's a water wave and electricity a moving charge, and magnetism, that's simple, it's just molecular magnets.

We cannot understand how things operate, how they move, how they are put together, unless we produce recall that specifically describes the cause of the effects we see.

With no requirement that we actually explain what is going on, once we have put a name to something we are free to make up anything we damn well please!

And because nonanswers produce understanding, because we think we understand when we see a falling object and recall gravity, because we think we understand when we see light and recall a wave, because we think we understand when we see the sun come up and recall angular momentum, we never experience the neuronic impacts that might call attention to the hole in our recall and we never question the defective explanation we have manufactured.

And because any answers that don't cause us pain are good enough, we come up with answers associated with our maker.

To the extent that we associate questions of force and motion with our maker, the technology we produce will not reflect reality and we will be deluded into thinking we can have no recall for questions the answers to which could be reflected in the technology we produce to extend our range of survivability in physical reality.

When Newton created his empirical scheme to prove that gravity was a property of matter, he left standing the religious belief that God created motion in the planets when the planets were formed, the same sort of religious belief, inertia, that Galileo had installed in the Earth to have it rotating in frictionless space. A century later, when it was realized that these religious beliefs were still permeating what was supposed to be objective measurements of physical reality and thus free of belief, Laplace concocted a swirling mass of gas to explain planetary orbiting and rotation, an occult belief that is solidly on the side of the gods but which is universally in recall to this day.

All of the words we make up as substitutes for our actually understanding how physical reality operates are mysticism hidden behind a belief in a bogus method that supposedly turns beliefs into facts.

But so long as everybody believes them to be facts, they are facts. When nobody believes anything else, recall is reality.

To the extent people don't realize that their recall does not reflect reality, they are deluded. Delusion is not bad on a personal basis because it shields us from neuronic impacts, allows our recall to provide answers to questions in reality for which we would otherwise have no answers.

However, delusion can retard progress by retarding the production of an accurate technology. The mind can only alter reality if it has an accurate picture of reality in recall to alter. If we do not have an accurate picture of physical reality in recall, then any attempt we make to alter reality will only alter it, if at all, to match our defective recall. If we have asked the question, what makes objects fall instead of the question what generates the force that makes objects fall, we expend all our efforts attempting to keep objects from falling and expend no effort dealing directly with the force itself.

If we do not have an accurate picture of physical reality in recall, we will not be able to effectively alter physical reality to our benefit and therefore produce accurate technology. Without accurate technology, technology that reflects reality, our ability to extend our range of survivability in physical reality will be limited.

With the failure to produce accurate pictures of reality, the technology we do produce will be misdirected. The by-product of technology, prosperity, produces commerce, the distribution of the benefits of technology. At the same time that prosperity is producing a ubiquitous "I" informed by Exalted Empathy, the need to help those less fortunate, it is also producing more of those less fortunate who desire the prosperity the technology produces and will seek to obtain it by force if necessary.

Thus, instead of directing our efforts at producing an accurate technology, we will direct our efforts at producing a technology that will allow us to protect our commerce or take the commerce of those more prosperous than ourselves.

We use the by-product of this operation of our mind, the ability to create realities that don't exist, to create the short term pleasure of commerce, short term because, without a consistent picture of physical reality upon which to produce an accurate technology, we make ourselves short term.

9. COMMERCE

Picture, please, a peaceful community that evolved in a pleasant valley that abounds in the nonambulatory animate matter that we cherish as fruits and nuts and grains and where the gentle hillsides are alive with the ambulatory animate matter whose roasting flesh affords our taste buds so many delights.

When the mantle of winter descends, however, the ground grows hard and the game ambulates to a more conducive clime.

During periods of plenty, provisions must be laid up against the long period between the seasons of plenty and, to accommodate this period of need, the residents of the valley have established a community warehouse to store their provisions

One year, at the end of the season of plenty, with provisions garnered for the coming season of need, a miscreant member of the community burns the warehouse down, the resulting conflagration destroying all of its contents, the game and grain, the fruits and nuts stored to ensure survival.

What's the community going to do with the guy that torched its food supply?

If the community is prosperous and has evolved to the point that it has nine percent whose ubiquitous "I"s have evolved from embodying "Thou-shalt-nots" to the dictates of Exalted Empathy so that their intellectual "I"s routinely form pictures of their external "I"s in the position of those less fortunate than themselves, no punishment is possible. The nine percent, being in a position of authority, could not mete out punishment because picturing any punishment would create a picture of their external "I"s in the position of those being punished, those less fortunate than themselves, and the picture would conflict with their intellectual "I"s. Attempting to punish others would in essence be an attempt to punish their external "I"s and the result would be the unendurable pain of neuronic impacts.

The major difference between the ubiquitous "I" informed by Golden Rule Behavior and the ubiquitous "I" informed by Exalted Empathy is that the ubiquitous "I" informed by Golden

Rule Behavior dictates that we forego acting out of the fear of the neuronic impacts recall of the acts might produce, while the ubiquitous "I" informed by Exalted Empathy dictates that we act in a certain way, make positive acts to help those less fortunate, or in the case of the miscreant that burned down the storehouse, rehabilitate him rather than decapitate him.

Attempting to punish produces neuronic impacts while not punishing feels good because it does not produce neuronic impacts.

Even though we have become inured to the pain that results from holding pictures of reality in recall that don't agree with reality and thus we can alter that reality, we cannot hold a picture in recall that causes our external "I"s pain when we can create a recall that shows us engaging in acts that would eliminate that pain. Because we place our external "I"s in situations that don't exist in reality to test how we are going to act in reality, when we have to choose between punishing and not punishing, the neuronic impacts from reflexively imagining our external "I"s as the object of the punishment make the choice for us and we eliminate the picture of the punishment if we can.

Mercy, relieving the potential object of punishment from the temporary personal discomfort, or worse, that the punishment would cause affords us a lifetime of pleasure because circumstances surrounding the act of mercy can be experienced in recall over and over for the rest of our lives.

If the awareness of the little valley society has reached the point at which authorities entrusted with enforcing behavior are informed by Exalted Empathy, then no punishment is possible, all violations of Golden Rule Behavior are tolerated and nothing would befall the miscreant that burned down the storage warehouse and destroyed all of the food.

On the other hand, the miscreant's behavior has endangered the community, possibly even brought it to an end. Without food, everybody will starve to death.

As the provisionless winter progresses, what might happen to the community's attitude toward punishment?

As the first pangs of hunger start to course through the enclave, current flows from the stomach begin to enter the mind and cause the mind to form pictures of honey loaves of bread and roasting legs of venison. Without any honey loaves of bread in reality and without any roasting legs of venison in reality, the pictures driven into the mind by hunger will have no counterpart in reality and the conflict of recall with reality will start to send neuronic impacts into the body, producing pain, personal punishment, undeserved torment.

To relieve the pain of these neuronic impacts, some members of the community, not, of course, those informed by Exalted Empathy whose position around wealth has allowed them to salt away some venison under the floorboards, and not those informed by Golden Rule Behavior because forming a picture of themselves carrying out the punishment would be a picture of themselves violating Golden Rule Behavior, but some members of the community will reflexively begin to banish their pain by forming pictures of the cause of their pain undergoing all the torments available in every circle of hell.

Our miscreant might be in trouble.

After the first elderly person dies, and the first baby's cries are drowned out by the silence of the skillets, thoughts of revenge might well become overpowering, so overpowering, in fact, that our miscreant might find himself the subject of a banquet at which he provides both the entertainment and the food.

We step in between a mad dog and its food at our own risk, and anyone without food becomes mad indeed. Cops quickly learn to wait until a couple finishes fornicating before arresting them for violating Golden Rule Behavior because Golden Rule Behavior is eliminated when demanding physical needs become overpowering.

Starvation reduces behavior, either Golden Rule Behavior or the behavior demanded by Exalted Empathy, to acts that fill the stomach!

If our peaceful community occupied a valley next to another valley and that other valley was inhabited by another peaceful community, then regardless of any cordial past relations between the communities, the community with provisions becomes at risk to the needs of our miscreant's community as soon as the miscreant burns down the community's warehouse.

There might be some negotiations.

The leaders of the first community, overcome by Exalted Empathy and revolted at the thought of taking another's provisions, might ask the members of the second community to share their provisions.

On the other hand, faced with their starving, ravenous members, the leaders of the first community might just as well attack the second community, pillage it of all its food, especially if they think they can get away with it, and, depending on want, even if they don't. To survive, the nine and the one might collude to go over the hill and, out of the recall of the ninety, away from any possibility of awareness on the part of the potential beneficiaries of their actions, do those things which are necessary, and more, to bring home the bacon.

Morality goes right out the window when the basic wants of food are in question and if our god remains, it is only as justification for the violations of Golden Rule Behavior we are driven to perform to satisfy our even greater pain. The conundrum of what we would do if me and thee were in the middle of the ocean with a life raft that would only support one of us is a product of idyll Exalted Empathy because animate matter, life, is basic and facing the absence of life is unendurable.

Contrary to the vacuous Janewayism from *Star Trek: Voyager*, a program whose technical innovations are inspired by the limitations imposed on physical reality by empirical fantasies, that "It is wrong to sacrifice another being to save our own lives!" there is no question what we would do. We would form a picture of our external "I"s on the raft and we would be driven by the neuronic impacts created by facing our nonexistence to do everything we could to make that picture a reality to keep ourselves animated.

One of us would go down!

Shelter is second only to food. The concentric circles formed by our recall dictates who will get into our fallout shelter, with those embedded in the most recall getting the choicest bunks and those not in recall, or, because recalling them causes us pain, those we refuse to recall being forced out into the cold canard of old, the nuclear winter.

As society grows more complex, food and shelter are not produced by the individual, or even the community, they are produced at a distance, and the process of moving food and shelter from its source to its consumption is commerce.

And, in a complex society, commerce has very little to do with food and shelter!

Food and shelter are survival needs and therefore, like sex, produce recall that is driven by the body and its needs.

These necessities are like the brick wall in reality. Our physical body hits the brick wall and bounces off.

No meaning required.

Without food and shelter and sex, we have no future, we cease to become animate matter. Faced with their loss, we become driven solely by neuronic impacts and therefore our acts cease to require meaning. Without meaning there is no need to explain existence, and there is no need to manufacture a god or morality, the Golden Rule Behavior we ascribe to our creator.

But there are a whole lot of things in this world other than food, shelter and sex, starting not in the least with the infinite variations of food, shelter and sex that produce a set of seven programmable deadly sins in the ubiquitous "I", prohibitions against envy and greed, gluttony and lust. Of the remaining deadly sins, sloth is either the sin of not contributing to the community or the result of gluttony and lust, and pride and anger usually lead to violations of Golden Rule Behavior.

While our needs are analogous to the brick wall in reality, we don't spend much of our time dwelling on them. If our needs are being satisfied, we continue to live. If they are not, we cease to exist.

On the other hand, our wants are analogous to authority in society. Authority, created where we abdicate our freedom of action or our willingness to produce answers concerning ourselves and the world we occupy, has no physical substance. However, authority is more real than reality itself because violations of authority cause real pain as a result of the neuronic impacts the contemplation of those violations produce.

Our wants also have no substance.

And they can also produce real pain.

However, the analogy between authority and our wants ends at this point. Authority is theoretically limited — it can only kill us — while our wants, solely a product of our recall, are limitless in scope. Because our wants are driven by neuronic impacts, the conflict of our external "I"s with something we don't have in reality, they are just as real as the authority we are driven to blindly obey.

The neuronic impacts unsatisfied wants produce makes those wants more real than reality itself because of the resulting pain.

Society can never produce enough to satisfy our wants because the reality that is the source of products that satisfy our wants is limited while the recall manufacturing those wants is limitless!

We do not want long our basic needs because without them we die, but our unfulfilled wants stay with us throughout our days.

Unfulfilled wants are even more tyrannical than authority because all we need to do to eliminate the neuronic impacts created by authority is to obey it.

The only way to relieve the neuronic impacts produced by not having what we want is to get what we don't have.

And the neuronic impacts that drive us to get what we don't have easily overpower the neuronic impacts authority programs into the ubiquitous "I".

Commerce is the process society evolves to satisfy the wants of its members. In complex societies, commerce becomes an institution, a system of procedures and technology that moves goods and services from their creation to their consumption.

Because commerce satisfies both the basic needs, food and shelter, and the myriad other wants generated by the collective recall of society, the satisfaction of which are more insistent than the satisfaction of the basic wants themselves, commerce becomes the single institution in society that cannot be attacked by any other.

When push comes to shove, the morality of the marketplace vill supersede Golden Rule Behavior!

We will fight and die for trade routes more readily than we will fight to impose our god and morality on others although we always claim the former to be the latter, and we will fight all gods and systems of morality, anything, in fact, that attempts to destroy our access to our trade routes.

Wants have their origin in the operation of the mind, in its function of comparing recall with reality. Technology, which is the precursor of prosperity, evolves as a result of this comparison process. We learn by watching others do. If someone stumbles upon a process to smelt bronze, then the process of smelting bronze becomes a series of pictures, serial recall, which can be demonstrated to others in physical reality. The pictures of smelting can be drawn or created with words in a book, but books only result in a wider dissemination of the process.

We learn processes by watching someone else carry out the processes. As we watch the other person carry out a process, we form pictures of our external "I"s carrying out the process, and we then encode those pictures as serial recall, storing the serial recall in our neuronic storage bins for future recall. When we want to smelt bronze, we start the recall process and serial recall takes us through the process by producing in recall a picture of our external "I"s smelting bronze and then we physically smelt the bronze in physical reality.

This is why we cannot unlearn something we have learned. We can grow old, our neuronic storage bins can harden and become inaccessible, the current level our brains generate may become imprecise and thus access all sorts of stuff, recall pictures of the blue Danube in the middle of the serial recall dealing with smelting bronze, and society itself can become fragmented, authority can destroy knowledge, or knowledge can become taboo resulting in later minds being ignorant of the process, or the value of the process might make it a secret of the temple, trampled upon only at the risk of trampling upon our god, but as long as things are functioning, as long as society is open and operating, we will recall what we have stored whether we want to or not.

We can not not recall what we have in mind!

Just as we watch someone performing an act and substitute our external "I"s performing the act, when we see someone in physical reality doing something or possessing something, we substitute our external "I"s doing or possessing that something, and we see how it agrees with our intellectual "I"s, with our experience of the things we like and dislike, the things that cause us pleasure and pain.

This is an automatic process that results from having the two evolutionary "I"s that society takes advantage of to instill Golden Rule Behavior. As we go through our days, we are constantly watching others, what they are wearing, how they walk, how they look, what they say, what they do and we are just as constantly forming a picture of our external "I"s wearing or looking or acting or possessing what we see in our recall. If we like the picture of the external "I" that we see, then we want to put ourselves, as Madison Avenue likes to say, in the driver's seat.

What we want can be possessions, including friends and lovers, or something less tangible, love, respect, or a combination of both, if I am thin I will be loved, if I have muscles, I will get respect.

When we see somebody with something that agrees with our intellectual "I"s when we recall a picture of our external "I"s possessing it, we form a picture of our external "I"s possessing it and store that picture in our recall. Every time we subsequently recall that picture, we have a conflict of our recall with reality, we have a recall of ourselves possessing something that we don't possess in reality.

We will receive neuronic impacts which we might interpret as envy.

We can illustrate the process by selecting a hat.

We go into a hat store and are overwhelmed by the variety of hats available for our head. We have just seen someone with a hat, call it a flat hat, and when we tried it on our external "I", it agreed with our intellectual "I", which is to say that the picture we saw in our recall pleased us, did not produce neuronic impacts.

In the store we see tall hats and short hats, wide hats and thin hats, open hats and closed hats, but we don't see any flat hats.

We have already gone through the process of buying hats, so we know that we like tall hats and we like wide hats, and we have plenty of both as a result, and we know we don't like open hats and closed hats, they cause us neuronic impacts when we picture them on our external "I", but now we want a flat hat and we ask the sales clerk if he has any flat hats.

He looks puzzled, and we describe what we have just seen on the street, use words to translate our recall into a picture that the sales clerk can use to poll his recall.

"Oh." he says, "you mean the new level headed approach to top wear. We just got a shipment in this morning. I'll bring a bunch up for you."

He disappears into the bowels of the store while we admire the thin hats, wondering if they could pass for flat hats if they were turned on their sides.

When the sales clerk returns, he has a variety of what we want stacked on his head and piled up on both upraised hands. He spreads them around for us to see.

At first we are faced with a pile of purple flimgasts, things for which we have no recall because we have never seen this style before today, and we are now seeing all sorts of variations of the new style. We have trouble categorizing them, but we know one way to categorize them and that's to put them on and look at ourselves in the mirror. We will then see our external "I" in actual reality with the hats on and we can compare one with the other by reference to the degree of neuronic impacts each produces.

We try one on and look first this way and that, set it aside and try on another one, and going through the same motions, still another and then another, and then we go back to the first, then a new one and then the third and then two new ones.

This is how we determine our wants, what pleases us, what, by not causing us pain, affords us pleasure.

When we finally decide on a particular flat hat, we can then buy it, which would mean that we could match reality with the recall we produced every time we wanted to see ourselves in the hat. Or, we might delay the purchase, which is to say, delay the gratification of satisfying our recall. Not having something that we know we can have produces mild neuronic impacts that can easily be interpreted as sexual in nature, so that delaying obtaining a want we have might well be more pleasing than immediately satisfying that want.

On the other hand, as we sit picturing ourselves without the hat we could easily acquire if we wanted, we might form a picture of the hat no longer available for purchase, the fad being of such immense proportions that all flat hats in the city will be bought up before the day has passed. In this case, we are left with a picture of our external "I" without the hat we want.

The neuronic impacts might be strong enough to send us grasping for our wallet.

And it is conceivable that we don't give a fig about hats at all. We could be walking down the street and see everybody in existence wearing flat hats and not even notice because we don't have any pictures of our external "I" in recall wearing any hat at all and have no interest in trying to form one.

We are oblivious to hats period.

Neuronic impacts produced by the relationship of experience with genetic disposition determine the multiplicity of wants that go into determining what goods and services flow through the channels of commerce.

Recall is not reality, can exist when there is no reality present, can be altered by altering the current levels associated with elements of the picture formed in recall, with virtually anything in recall being capable of being mixed and matched with anything else. With no physical limitations on recall, virtually any recall is possible, and because we always form a picture of our external "I"s in recall, any picture of our external "I"s with anything imaginable can be created and stored in recall. When that picture is later recalled, it will conflict with the picture of ourselves in physical reality, our actual external "I"s, and the resulting neuronic impacts will drive us to match physical reality with recall.

If we form a picture of our external "I"s wearing the Hope Diamond, we will be discontent when we wake up and find ourselves without the Hope Diamond!

The same thing happens when we watch a sporting event and see the stunning catch that wins the game with three seconds left, the catcher being carried off the field to the approving roar of the crowd and the popping of Asti Spumante corks. We form a picture of our external "I"s at the orgasmic moment of the catch and play it over and over, the imaginary cheers more real than reality in our recall washing over us wave after wave after wave only to wake up to the reality that we are a kid in front of a television set. Once in recall, however, the picture replays itself over and over, driving us to try and duplicate it in reality. If instead of a catch, it is a winning basket, we are on the basketball court making the shot over and over in our minds regardless of what is happening in reality. We are making our body come as close as possible to the reality in our recall as we can, even to the point of duplicating the shorts and shoes that inspired the recall.

Fashion and sports are about as far away from food and shelter as we can get, but as a society becomes more prosperous, they take on a much greater share of the wants generated within that society and thus capture a greater proportion of the commerce the society generates.

But they by no means delimit the range of wants a society generates.

Which presents prosperous societies with a difficult problem.

While it is not every member of society that can look at someone smelting bronze and store an accurate enough picture of the process in serial recall to allow their external "I"s to smelt bronze, everyone that sees a picture of people basking on the shores of some exotic isle halfway around the world can produce a picture of their external "I"s basking on the beach, and recall that picture over and over at will.

The ability of recall to produce wants in unlimited amounts, combined with a prosperous society that creates goods and services in an abundance far beyond the possibility of any one individual accessing them all when mixed with communications systems that create pictures of all the wants available accessible to all the members of the society results in the production of wants far in excess of the supply of goods and services that are available to satisfy those wants.

Even if some sort of distribution system could be devised that would distribute goods and services without reference to the contributions of the consumers of those goods and services to their production and distribution, an unrealized goal of the prosperity produced by the replacement of labor by technology, at some point the production of the goods and services, with no limit on their consumption, will outstrip the ability of the environment to continue to produce them.

With little respect for those that forcefully and endlessly argue that there are no limits to growth that technology cannot overcome, the reality based on the mechanical way the mind operates is that, with unlimited wants, there is no technology possible that can satisfy the wants of the society producing the commerce attempting to satisfy those wants.

Prosperity creates widespread leisure time which means that our recall is not functioning full time to move our external "I"s through physical reality. We have time to contemplate the nature of that physical reality, and in the process, to create wants with respect to that physical reality.

With the resulting wants going unsatisfied, a sort of background static of neuronic impacts is always present in the members that make up a prosperous society, with the level of neuronic impacts varying from group to group within the society depending on how successful each group is in satisfying its wants in comparison with other groups. This is an unrecognized level of pain that is interpreted as anxiety and shortens the gap between compliance with the considerably liberalized behavioral prohibitions programmed into the ubiquitous "I" and outright violations of Golden Rule Behavior.

Society always organizes itself to protect itself, which means to protect its members, so that as long as society is capable of organization, it will take the steps necessary to ensure that the behavior of its members does not get out of control.

But one thing that society will not do and can not do is to disrupt the established channels of commerce. Regardless of the number of wants that are going unsatisfied in a society, to the extent that wants are being satisfied, the neuronic impacts that would occur if those wants were denied will far outstrip any neuronic impacts occurring as a result of unrealized wants that have never been satisfied.

Just as being told not to have sex is a poor bar to not having sex when sex offers itself, so the denial of unsatisfied wants produces minor neuronic impacts when compared to the denial of wants that are accustomed to being satisfied.

This results because the recall that contains a picture of the external "I" with unsatisfied wants merely conflicts with a picture of reality that, while it exists, is not a bar to moving through physical reality where those wants have never been satisfied. If we have a picture of ourselves with a car and we have never had a car, then we will be resentful as we ride the bus, but we will still be able to move through physical reality. We only have recall of something that never existed.

Yearning for a mother we never had is not the same as suffering the loss of a mother we always had.

If we have always had a car, however, every picture we have of self, every picture of our intellectual "I"s we have in recall contains a picture of our external "I"s having a car. Being deprived of the car has the same physical effect as losing a parent because the loss leaves a hole in our recall that will be with us wherever we go.

However, while losing a parent might crush us, there is nothing we can do about it. We can damn well, and will do something about the loss of our car!

The old saw that satisfied wants become necessities, what was once a dream becomes a need, is the result of the incessant neuronic impacts caused by the holes in our recall, with our recall continually not matching reality when our realized wants go unsatisfied.

There is no greater societal benefit than the movement of goods and services in response to the needs of society and while prosperity creates the repose that produces both the multiplicity of wants and the tolerant views that prevent effective punishment for violations of Golden Rule Behavior, in complex societies any disruption of trade routes will invite instant retribution because, with the distance between the source and the consumption so great, nothing can be allowed to interfere with the movement of the goods and services to the consumer to satisfy the consumer wants.

Returning to our pleasant valley community, our miscreant might well have survived for awhile after he torched the community's food supplies, and if he were wily enough, he might well redirect the community's rage at the sister community over the hill, becoming the chief proponent of pillage as a cure for the hunger pains and a substitute for revenge.

The miscreant may well have been one of the "one"s of the ninety, nine and one who, having realized that population pressures required annexation of the sister community's resources to preserve the continually increasing needs of his own community, burned the food supplies to stir the nine into an action that would merely serve to satisfy the needs of the ninety.

Even in a society in which the ubiquitous "I" is informed by Exalted Empathy, no matter how great our reverence for life and no matter how we think we can avoid punishment by rehabilitation, anything that gets between us and our Calvins is going to be dead meat!

10. CONFLICT

Although the following scenario is frightening, it cannot occur because gravity is a property of and therefore proportional to mass, the matter that produces the gravity. A planetary body is incapable of changing its mass. Because a change in mass could never occur, the change in gravity necessary to produce the scenario could never occur.

Therefore, the scenario never occurred and the empirical praetorians, schooled in fantasy, can throw the fagots back on the woodpile.

Gravity, of course, is merely the concept we made up and placed in recall to avoid the neuronic impacts that would otherwise occur every time we saw an object fall. To avoid the pain of not knowing, of not comprehending, we have created a word to recall and mindlessly compare with what we see, tricking ourselves into believing that we understand what we see, why the object is falling.

The evolution of scientific nonsense into concrete reality is illustrated by the Smithsonian's recently revised exhibit dealing with the origin of the solar system which is housed at the National Museum of Natural History in Washington D.C. Before the exhibit's revision, the wall chart laying out the design of the solar system cautioned that it was only *thought* that the solar system condensed out of a swirling mass of gas.

The revised exhibit gives a detailed time line plotting the step by step process of solar system formation accompanied by actual photographs.

We have taken our fantasies and made them a reality in our recall!

The evolution of gravity from concept to fact, on the other hand, occurred in the last century, which left the scientific establishment in this century to argue the theoretical effects of gravity, the nature of event horizons in black holes and the missing matter holding galaxies together.

The only question about solar system formation left as far as the Smithsonian is concerned appears to be whether the solar system condensed out of a left hand or right hand swirl of gas.

The notion that objects fall as a result of a property originated from a series of conceptual mistakes set out in the seventh volume of The Copernican Series, *Where Science Went Wrong* and those conceptual mistakes have been compounded by putting one occult belief after another into recall, with each in turn taking on the appearance of fact. With so many concepts accepted as fact piled atop one another, to contradict the mass/gravity concept is to contradict what is believed to be, not an established fact in reality, but reality itself.

"Gravity is not a property of matter" is heard by the initiate as "there is no force that makes objects fall" and the catechism "Walk up to the top of the Empire State Building and jump, and I'll guarantee you will realize that there is a force that makes objects drop!" is the rote response.

The belief in the mass/gravity concept is so basic that people cannot draw a distinction between the fact that objects drop and the fact that there might be more than one explanation for why objects drop.

When people were making up the laws dealing with falling objects, they were operating in total ignorance about such universal facts as electricity and its concomitant inductances, or the fact that the center of planets, and the surfaces of some planets are warm, even hot. Had these dead men who knew nothing been aware of the fact that planets were hot and therefore emitted heat in what we today call electromagnetic radiation, they still would have had to be able to draw a parallel between two facts.

The first fact is that an emission field, electromagnetic radiation, light, expands over the surface of an expanding sphere which diminishes inversely with the square of its distance from the source.

The second fact deals with the force that makes objects fall. This force causes falling objects to accelerate at a measured rate that increases with the square of the distance over which they fall.

This means that the force causing objects to fall diminishes at the same rate that emissions expand, inversely with the square of distance.

Because modern science has yet to make this rather obvious connection, it is doubtful that the dead men who made up mass/gravity, had they known more than the little they did know, would have been able to make the connection.

Even had these dead men made the connection, they probably would have been prevented from considering the fact that the force of attraction had something to do with expanding emission fields by the neuronic impacts such a consideration would create in themselves, and the rage those neuronic impacts would produce in others against the person suggesting such an absurdity.

And yet, that is not only what I am suggesting, it is what happens in physical reality!

With the attractive force a product (as opposed to the occult nonexplanation "property") of a planet's cooling process and proportional to the rate of that cooling process, the planet's temperature, then the force that makes objects fall is not only a dynamic current force that actually exists in physical reality and does something in that physical reality, it is a force that changes over time.

The sun is very hot, has a very strong emission field and thus exerts a very strong force of attraction. Jupiter, cooler than the sun and therefore having less of an attractive force, is by far the hottest of the planets, being classified a proto-star, and has the strongest attractive force of any planet. The Earth has cooled off so that its force of attraction is smaller than Jupiter's, but stronger than the attractive force of Mars which, half the size of the Earth, is cooler than the Earth, while the moon, a hunk of rock that has cooled off totally on its surface, doesn't have much of an attractive force at all.

But that doesn't mean that the moon wasn't hot at one time!

There is no reason to look out at the planets and assume that the solar system is made up of anything but matter that was formed at approximately the same time, combusted at the same time, and is cooling off at the same rate, with the smaller planets cooling off sooner than the larger planets which still have stronger emission fields and thus correspondingly stronger fields of attraction.

Because an attractive force resulting from emission fields would be holding the solar system together against the forces trying to tear it apart as opposed to the current view, where the instability measured in the solar system is considered to be the result of historical forces exactly balancing the dynamics of the system, it's cohesion being a product of blind, dumb luck, rather than current forces — blind, dumb luck in turn being analogous to the mystical mass that produces the occult gravity which diminishes when it doesn't perform work, but doesn't when it does — latecomers to the system, like comets or even small planets, would be capable of being incorporated into the system without destroying the system's stability. A planet such as Venus, too hot for its size to have been formed as a part of the system, could well be such a latecomer.

Knowing that the planets formed hot and cooled as matter cools on Earth, with the larger objects taking longer to cool than the smaller objects, we would know that the Earth's small moon had simply cooled off.

But knowing that the Earth's moon could cool off before the Earth because of its smaller size would also allow us to know that the moon probably evolved the same way that the Earth and other planets evolved, moons merely being planets that circle other planets rather than the sun.

Because the Earth has an atmosphere, we could conclude that the moon evolved with an atmosphere.

The primary product of an atmosphere is water, the marriage of the two abundant elements, hydrogen and oxygen, into their stable form.

Water, in turn, means oceans.

It is fairly simple to look at the moon with the naked eye and see the seabeds that cover its surface. The seabeds are actually named seabeds because they look like seas that have lost their water. Mare, Latin for sea, precedes the names of the principal geological features of the moon, with Mare Tranquillitatis, The Sea of Tranquility being the most famous.

There is even an ocean, Oceanus Procellarum between Mare Humorum and Mare Imbrium

Accompanying the appearance of emptied seabeds on the moon there is overwhelming evidence, embodied in the over four hundred and fifty flood stories from every society on Earth which include the Biblical flood story of Western tradition, and embedded on the physical surface of the planet, paleontological evidence, bone islands in Arctic ice flows and bone plugs in caves from North America to the Mediterranean and geographical evidence, cities buried beneath the Pacific from Japan to Pohnpei and erratics, huge boulders transported thousands of mile from their geologic source, that a large amount of water arrived on Earth at some time in the past from an external source.

Using erratics, the dislocation of the huge boulders that could only be accomplished by water, we have created a story in our recall that the Earth periodically produces ice ages that cause huge ice sheets to march from the North Pole down to around the fortieth parallel to manufacture comprehension about how these boulders moved and we accept this recall even though erratics appear high up in mountains where no ice sheets can climb and in the middle of deserts where no ices sheets extended, and against absolute evidence that ice sheets, other than glaciers which move from the weight of accumulated snow and ice down gullies to the sea, do not move over the surface of the Earth, cannot move up the sides of mountains, and absolutely don't travel thousands of miles over rocky terrain.

However, once we have produced this picture of traveling ice sheets falling down from the "top" of the planet in our recall, the picture being totally imaginary, unmatchable in reality, we maintain it in the face of opposition from its impracticality, that there is absolutely no explanation why or how such an event could occur, let alone occur on a repetitive basis. Unlike authority, which attempts to mirror the needs of the society producing it, scientific fantasies are fettered only by the willingness of a small group of individuals invested with the authority to provide answers for questions raised by physical reality to actually expend the mental energy to come up with answers that explain rather than put words without meaning to facts without meaning to produce meaning, which means that mindless scientific fantasies are not fettered at all, and by the public's willingness to suspend disbelief in the face of irrational pronouncements which carry with them the stamp of consensual approval, a willingness that, as a result of the neuronic impacts produced by opposing consensual dogma, doesn't exist.

When we look at the moon we have a picture of a dead, cold planet with massive markings on it showing that it once held water and on Earth we have overwhelming evidence that it obtained a lot of water from some other place.

Why don't we just conclude that the water which at some point in the past flooded the Earth came from the moon?

Because we have adopted a mystical belief in what makes objects fall, that it is the occult result of the existence of matter which somehow, although there is no evidence as to how, or even that it does, causes other matter to be attracted to it.

When we accept that a force that can cause motion is the same as a color like gold that can delight, a property of something, then for the amount of gravity to change, the amount of matter has to change.

We can look at the moon and see that there is not a big bite taken out of one side. If there is not a big bite taken out of one side, then the moon must have had the same amount of matter today that it had when it was formed, and as God installed the attractive force when He created the matter and the attractive force is therefore proportional to the amount of matter, with all of the moon that was ever there still there, any water on the moon that was ever there must still be there.

Because there is no water on the moon, then there was never any water on the moon, markings on the moon are just imagination and the uniform flood stories passed down in all historical accounts of the Earth are a sort of Jungian delusion created by the structure of the mind, whatever that structure might be, probably the portion that is hidden mystically in the subconscious, and the piles of bones, many mingling extinct species with present day species simply don't exist, the underwater Pacific ports are tourist attractions and the ice ages, historically correct facts that moved the erratics across the face of the Earth.

Because history doesn't exist, we can only look at the remains of what was, what we have left of history — myth, tradition and physical evidence as embodied in the remains of life and the distortions of the geographical picture — to piece together a narrative of what occurred in the past.

However, if we cripple our recall by creating facts that don't exist, the belief that the force of attraction is some sort of mystical property of matter that doesn't exist between its source and its effect other than, perhaps, as a space/time warp, but can still move huge boulders to crush us like ants, and then use those beliefs to limit our attempts to come up with a coherent narrative that explains the information we do have, we end up with a self-referential narrative in which all of the facts are actually beliefs made up to support the other beliefs, and none of the real facts in physical reality, the facts we have to use to create a consistent narrative that will tell us something about ourselves and the world we occupy, will be included, will in fact be held to be anomalies not worthy of explanation and thus ignored.

There is a narrative that ties the existing facts and myths together and that narrative has had a very real impact on the human behavior we find ourselves with on this particular planet in this particular solar system on the edge of the galaxy of which we are a part, and it is an effect that may be rather unique as planetary histories go.

If planets form and cool off at a uniform rate, then the Earth was much hotter at a specific point in the past. This would mean that much of the surface heat of the planet was derived from the emissions from the fiery core receding beneath its surface as it cooled off producing, along with the advent of animate matter, a tropical environment.

In a tropical environment plants would grow more rapidly and more abundantly than they do in today's cooler environment.

With the strength of the attractive force proportional to the rate of cooling, a hotter planet would have produced a stronger force of gravity requiring animals to have bones of immense size in order to move about.

As the planet cooled, smaller species evolved leading to our ancestors who in an environment made warm as a result of the internal heat of the Earth, had plentiful food and little need for shelter. We had very little need to fight for food.

In such an environment when we espy a succulent piece of fruit hanging from a branch, we form a picture in our recall of our external "I" picking the fruit and eating it.

We follow our external "I" over to the tree, reach up, grab the fruit, take it in hand and enjoy its sweet juices.

Tired, we fall asleep under the eucalyptus tree.

If we didn't rest our mind, the electrical flows that operated our recall would become less precise as the wet works that produced them became overworked, and without accurate electrical flows to match recall with reality we would find ourselves forming inaccurate pictures of reality, and with inaccurate pictures of reality in recall, missing our step, stumbling, in danger of falling and hurting ourselves.

The fruit provides us with the energy we need to get the old mind fired up with accurate electric flows so that, with pinpoint recall, we can go out and get ourselves another piece of fruit.

As long as we move unhindered through physical reality, we have no conflict, we have no problem procuring the fruit. If the fruit was way high up on the tree, and if we couldn't climb the tree, or we didn't know how to make a ladder, we might be prevented by physical reality from getting the fruit, and if we eat all of the fruit that we can reach and there is no more, we might cease to exist, but as long as nothing in physical reality conflicts with the pictures of our external "I" getting and eating the fruit, we will get the fruit and survive.

Conflicts with physical reality, the out-of-reach fruit, is one reason that we develop technology, the ladder. We use technology to overcome obstacles in reality so that we can continue to exist, even extend our range of survivability, in that reality.

But there is another source of conflict in external reality.

If we form a picture of our external "I" reaching for the fruit at the same time that another intellectual "I" attached to another organism in physical reality is forming a picture of its external "I" reaching for the same piece of fruit, we have a conflict in physical reality.

We have two intellectual "I"s forming identical pictures of their external "I"s and only one of those external "I"s is going to be able to match recall, a picture of his external "I" possessing the fruit, with reality, the organism actually possessing the fruit.

The intellectual "I" that ends up with the fruit will continue to form pictures of his external "I" eating the fruit and will suffer no neuronic impacts.

The intellectual "I" whose external "I" ends up without the fruit is going to have a picture in recall, his external "I" with the fruit, that doesn't agree with reality, his external "I" without the fruit.

If it is our external "I" that gets the fruit, then our adversary will have a conflict that will result in neuronic impacts which he will interpret as rage. As he tries to form a picture in recall that agrees with reality, the only picture that agrees with his hunger pains is a picture of his external "I" with our fruit, so serial recall produces a picture of his external "I" getting our fruit and he whacks us up side our head and takes our fruit.

We, of course, are forming a picture of our external "I" eating the fruit so that the whack up side our head takes us completely by surprise, stopping our minds from operating, sending massive neuronic impacts into our subsystems, and we lash out blindly in response, trying to protect both ourselves and our fruit.

When two intellectual "I"s form a picture of their external "I"s possessing the same thing in physical reality, then we are going to end up with a conflict that produces neuronic impacts because both organisms cannot possess or consume the same thing at the same time. If we are both driven by hunger pains, and those hunger pangs are greater than the neuronic impacts produced by not having possession, we will, unless we are *Voyager's* Janeway, fight to the death to take possession.

Conflict is simply the product of the way our minds function to first form pictures in response to bodily needs that show us satisfying those bodily needs, and then having those pictures opposed in physical reality, producing more neuronic impacts which drive us to turn the opposing pictures into reality. Necessity is certainly the mother of invention, and when we are prevented from eating our fruit, when we find the guy that whacked us up side the head is an oversized behemoth, we might just pick up a rock to equalize the transaction.

But the process, the agreement or disagreement of recall with reality that leads to physical conflict with others in external reality is built into the mind's operation. Behavior that leads to physical confrontation is produced by, is, in fact, driven by the neuronic impacts, the actual physical pain produced in our subsystems by the opposing pictures produced when physical reality, or others in physical reality oppose the pictures we form as a result of our basic needs, our requirement first for food, then for shelter and then for sex.

In a warm environment that produced rapid regeneration of food and therefore plentiful subsistence, a virtual paradise, conflict would be at a minimum because when two intellectual "I"s formed a picture of their external "I"s reaching for the same piece of fruit, and one got there a millisecond after the other, it would simply be easier to refocus the external "I" on the piece of fruit next to the one that was lost than it would be to form pictures that would lead to smacking someone up side the head.

Prosperity, at least when it comes to organisms whose only want is to fill their bellies, eliminates conflict, and in fact, in our own real world, if prosperity were limitless, and all wants could be satisfied, there would never be any conflict.

However, the notion that we could satisfy all wants is a fantasy on a par with the notion of mass/gravity.

There's always going to be conflict about who to bed, which might be one reason why sex is at the basis of the loss of paradise in the myths and traditions and there will always be conflict about resources because the pictures of recall that we can produce are limitless and the physical reality producing those resources is limited.

There will never be enough to go around and as a result there will always be conflict.

But if we assume that civilization grew up on Earth during a period when the Earth's climate was warmer, a pretty inescapable assumption, then the conflicts that arose would not have been over food, because food was one thing that would have been plentiful.

What would happen to such a civilization if, one fine morning, an amount of water equal to about five feet of the surface area of the Earth were dumped on it?

The civilization would not just find itself under water, it would find itself wiped out, with only scattered remnants surviving.

But worse, when the waters had settled into new oceans and seas, the additional weight pushing up new mountains at new ocean margins, the normal cooling process of the Earth would have been accelerated with an additional layer of matter piled on what was already a receding ball of fire beneath its surface. The emissions passing through this new layer to the Earth's surface would therefore be weaker, reducing the strength of the gravity holding the matter to the surface of the Earth, sounding the death knell for big-boned animate matter..

More important, the temperature the emissions had produced, making the climate warmer, would be lessened.

With the planet's internal source of heat lessened, the planet's surface would grow colder. Hydrogen and oxygen breaking down at the equator under the direct line of the sun's rays would convect north and south toward the poles where, out of the direct line of the sun's heat, they would precipitate out as snow and ice, forming the polar ice caps.

However, without question, the most devastating result of such a catastrophe would be the elimination of food from the environment causing the survivors to be driven by the neuronic impacts from unsatisfied hunger pains to form pictures of each other as food, resulting in the widespread cannibalism found in tradition following the flood myths.

With a cooler climate, less land mass and encroaching ice fields, food would never again be in abundance, and, while Golden Rule Behavior would eventually result in the elimination of cannibalism, the Earth would be filled with intellectual "I"s forming pictures of their external "I"s reaching for the same piece of fruit when there were no other pieces of fruit available.

No single society could form under such circumstances, but individual societies would form around the remaining fertile areas still capable of producing food.

However, because those food resources would never be sufficient to feed a growing society, all individual societies would eventually come into conflict with one another for each other's resources.

A civilization which would have normally been driven by Golden Rule Behavior to organize over a leisurely period of time into a single society as the slowly cooling planet produced a dwindling food supply was fractured, perhaps irretrievably, into societal segments, each in competition with the other for survival, and thus in constant conflict.

This narrative is based on a solid foundation, even down to the geographical evidence as to which direction the flood waters spilled over and left their mark on the surface of the Earth. But as compelling as the geographical evidence is, as confirmatory as the oral tradition is, and as inevitable as the physical outcome is from the dynamic nature of the attractive force, the psychological scars that remain as a result the catastrophe provide the ever present evidence of the event.

Under normal circumstances, inquiry into the nature of physical reality would proceed with the desire to be informed by that physical reality as to its operation. Having been reduced to the level of operating in simple response to neuronic impacts to survive, survivors knit their individual civilizations back together with a profound fear of the gods that created matter, assigning to the realm of their god all aspects of physical reality including those dealing with the nature of matter and its movement. Bits and pieces of knowledge that survived dictated the nature of all subsequently acquired knowledge, with an overpowering regard for water, the force of destruction, which became the explanation for light, the very thing by which we see physical reality.

As a result, in the approximately seven millennium intervening, we know absolutely nothing about the nature of heat or light, electricity or magnetism, we don't have a clue as to what holds the solar system together or what makes the planets and moons rotate and orbit, and we don't even attempt to come up with an explanation for why objects fall.

Afraid of angering the gods that destroyed us once before, we dare only peek obliquely at physical reality, coming up with occult explanations that, because they hide actual meaning from us, make us believe we are successfully hiding our search for meaning from our gods, who, if they found out we actually wanted to understand how physical reality operates, might rise up and smite us once again.

With no science, no knowledge, no understanding, no comprehension of what is actually occurring in physical reality, and no plans to even make an attempt at finding out, we resort to brute trial and error explorations into developing technologies that will allow us to take the food off the tables of the other societies with which we co-exist on a planet quickly growing cold and passing the range of survivability of its inhabitants, who, having missed the proverbial boat in reality, will probably die with the planet as it takes on the aspect of the moon that, like a fortuneteller pointing a bony finger to the future, circles it.

The subsequent history of the Earth has been one of using the recall process to produce pictures of reality that contain instruments of war that will allow one group to conquer and subject another to obtain the other group's food, its labor, and its physical resources to increase the prosperity of the conquering group. Virtually all technology that has not been centered around the production of food has gone into the production of instruments of war, of vehicles capable of offensive movement and of structures capable of defensive safety.

The record is fairly clear that copper weapons provided the first capability for widespread conquest of competing societies, but with the discovery that alloying tin with copper made bronze, bronze weapons took over the world which at the time spread out around the Mediterranean.

Europe, Asia and Africa had little tin, however, with neither the geological nor historical record showing evidence of tin mining on these accessible land masses that would account for the massive amounts that went into the production of the Bronze Age. Evidence of massive tin mining, on the other hand, does exist in abundance in North and South America, and these tin mining operations were all located near copper deposits so that t\

he process of alloying bronze occurred on site with the completed bronze transported to the Mediterranean by the mysterious Peoples of the Sea.

These people who settled in as the Phoenicians after the iron age replaced the Bronze Age became fabulously wealthy as they plied the ocean between the Mediterranean and the Americas, their mystery born of the necessity to maintain absolute secrecy about the navigational skills that were at the basis of the trade routes that produced the wealth of the bronze whose control purchased the world.

The establishment of these secret and highly guarded trade routes to ship bronze from the new world saw the establishment of trade routes from the west and the establishment of overland or coastal trade routes to the east. Vast empires in the Americas grew up around the wealth that flowed from the coffers of the conquered societies around the Mediterranean and the remains of these empires dot the Americas to this day.

However, when advanced smelting technology produced iron and then steel, the bronze age ended and the trade routes to the west dried up, isolating these societies, the resulting disappearance providing an enduring example of what happens when wealthy societies informed by Exalted Empathy face dwindling resources with expanding populations.

The Bronze Age established the importance of commerce to the affairs of nations who wished to dominate others to their own prosperity rather than be dominated to the prosperity of others. Trade routes and their protection, self-protection, preemptive strikes for self-preservation and strikes for looting drove the technology we developed.

Instead of attempting to figure out the nature of physical reality and focus our efforts on changing that physical reality to ensure our survival, we focused our attention on hiding our trade routes, lying about our technology to confuse our enemies and producing instruments of war that could destroy the competition.

Because technology is a two-edged sword and therefore requires secrecy, the procedures under which technology was developed were separated and the people developing the technology worked with blinders on. With blinders, isolated islands of knowledge evolved, and with that isolation, shared realities as to what reality was. These shared realities produced coteries whose vision was forced inward and made reliant on consensus agreement to carry forward their tasks, fracturing the search for answers to the questions raised by the operation of physical reality into authoritative specialties ignorant of the general knowledge required to effectively analyze questions of motion and force.

The alloying of secrecy with the confusion over which areas of physical reality involved questions for which there can be no recall drove people to mistake the search for technology with efforts to divine the secrets of the universe in order to produce weapons that would lead to universal domination. The authority granted to the coteries that grew up around the process of making up narratives dealing with these secrets centered in a self-perpetuating consensus that admitted only those that agreed with the consensus and excluded those that challenged it.

Because the consensus answers to the questions were beyond absurdity, space, something that can be warped and folded over on itself, time, a measurement that can be speeded up or slowed down, gravity, a property, magnetism, molecular magnets, electricity a moving charge, light not even something, but like something, a water wave, and heat, not the same as the light, had no relation to reality, and because the authorities charged with creating knowledge about motion and force and the nature of matter were so lazy and ignorant and afraid of retribution by the gods they were challenging that they could only come up with patent absurdities, the absurdities posited as narratives of reality had to be justified with the claim that the series of silly concepts were derived objectively by a procedure that turned fantasy into fact, and that the entire technology, produced in desperation of death by trial and error efforts in the face of impending destruction by marching armies and unrelated to the absurd narrative, actually resulted from the narrative, the occult bullcrap being presented as fact, the claim that mass/gravity produced jet planes and that the concepts of electricity and magnetism produced television sets, the endless malassociations of concept with technology that pervade all of empirical science.

The cycle is driven by neuronic impacts. Because neuronic impacts are inherent in the operation of the mind, the cycle is inherent in the interaction of human beings so long as there are disparate societies.

A group of people form into a society to protect their food resources and their shelter. The society grows too large for its food resources and the society needs to take the food resources of its neighbors, or it lives next to neighbors who have outgrown their food resources and needs to defend itself and its food resources, and its shelters from those neighbors. Pictures formed in member's recall show members positioned at various points in the concentric circles of their recall being killed or starving and the resulting neuronic impacts drive them to take whatever advantage they can to survive and improve their position. Different groups of people combine to further their own interests, their individual survival, but only so long as there isn't a clear advantage to use the combination to obtain additional advantage, as an opportunity to destroy their ally and take their resources.

In seven thousand years, we have slowly moved back toward a position in which there will be only a single society on the face of the Earth, a position that, if reached, will reduce conflicts to questions of who goes to bed with whom and which football team takes home the trophy.

And we will be attempting to do so with a superstitious set of beliefs we claim as science, as real knowledge, which are so inculcated into our recall that even thinking of alternatives is enough to drive us to rage or ridicule but which limits our picture of physical reality and therefore limits the technology we might devise to extend our range of survivability in that physical reality, a physical reality that is growing colder by the day as evidenced by the measurable rise of the oceans which is not, as popularly believed, produced by the ice caps melting as a result of the planet growing hot in the deep, dark cold of space, but rather is produced by the reduction in the strength of the gravity which, being proportional to the rate of cooling, becomes less as the planet becomes colder, uncompressing the water as it does so, causing it to rise in the ocean beds.

In the meantime, our societies have consistently sent their members out to rape, torture, main, enslave and kill members of other societies.

Such acts violate Golden Rule Behavior, the glue that holds societies together!

It is this need to survive, to violate Golden Rule Behavior to prosper and populate, that produces the ninety, nine and one, the exact proportion of the numbers perhaps conceptual, but the actual division very real, because the existence of society depends on a proportion of its members willing to violate Golden Rule Behavior to benefit the many.

11. THE NEED TO VIOLATE GOLDEN RULE BEHAVIOR

In spite of recent, extremely bloody attempts to prove otherwise in the countries that made up the communist block of nations, private property is at the basis of the social contract. The condition of these fractured societies, economic basket cases all, memorializes the reality that the possession of property flows naturally from the operation of the mind.

The societal basis of private property is apparent in the mind's operation.

When we have a shiny diamond, we form a picture of our external "I"s possessing the shiny diamond. If someone takes the diamond from us, we are left with a picture in recall of ourselves possessing the diamond and a reality in which we don't possess the diamond. The resulting neuronic impacts stay with us until we can return reality to recall, regain physical possession of the diamond. The actions we will form in our recall of our external "I"s regaining possession of the diamond are limited only by the pain we feel from the neuronic impacts we get from not having the diamond.

When we have had the diamond all of our lives, then having the diamond becomes as much a part of our recall as our self, and not having the diamond is an attack on self, an attack that produces a violent reaction, anger, revenge, a holy crusade to regain the diamond.

This applies whether we are dealing with diamonds, the land that produces our food, our shelter, and even our family members, the people that occupy the inner concentric circles of our recall.

Protecting our own is basic because when we are deprived of our own we have a hole in our recall. Part of the picture we have of ourselves, part of our picture of self in recall, no longer exists in reality.

Society recognizes the importance of objects in physical reality that make up the inner concentric circles of our recall, protecting those objects by defining Golden Rule Behavior and classifying violations of Golden Rule Behavior as either religiously or civilly proscribed.

We cannot take another's property because to do so would create a hole in that person's recall which would result in that person experiencing neuronic impacts which would drive him to revenge the taking of his property.

Society cannot form if its members are continually engaged in righting old wrongs.

The first task of society is to prohibit the wrongs and the second task of society is to create a system for redressing the wrongs that do occur to minimize the neuronic impacts caused by those wrongs and thus the additional wrongs those neuronic impacts might produce.

Golden Rule Behavior is programmed into the members of society by example either through religious parables incorporating vivid pictures of hellfire and damnation for acts that violate Golden Rule Behavior, by civil proclamations combined with very real current and public punishments for those violations or by a combination of both.

These behavioral prohibitions fight fire with fire. They take advantage of the way the mind operates to produce neuronic impacts, the production of pain when visualizing potential pictures of punishment, to protect society from the way that the mind operates when it is faced with the neuronic impacts that result from the desire to possess what it doesn't possess or from the present loss of possession, the retaliatory response to pain that can tear society apart

Not having another's property produces neuronic impacts that drive us to take another's property. Having others take our property produces neuronic impacts that drive us to seek revenge.

Society produces recall designed to punish the taking of property by inculcating pictures of punishments that cause sufficient neuronic impacts to drive out any thoughts of taking another's property and if someone still takes another's property, steps in to administer punishment so the member whose property was taken won't be driven by neuronic impacts to seek revenge, killing two birds with one stone by using the punishment to discourage future takings.

Having our possessions taken and wanting the possessions of others produces identical responses in different degrees.

When we see someone else with something we don't have, we form a picture of ourselves having it, and the resulting conflict, not having in reality what we see our external "I"s having in recall, also produces pain. Because we have never actually possessed what we covet, we don't have actual recall of possession. The resulting neuronic impacts are therefore weaker than the neuronic impacts produced by losing something we possess.

Society utilizes the weakness of the neuronic impacts produced by recalling our external "I"s with possessions that are not attached to our intellectual "I"s. It uses the mind's ability to produce a recall that might exist, the potential of punishment, to create stronger neuronic impacts to help us overcome the neuronic impacts that result from coveting what we don't have.

The stronger neuronic impacts produced by recalling pictures of punishment drown out the weaker neuronic impacts produced by not possessing that which we don't yet have.

If we can associate having our hand cut off with taking another's property, and we have actually seen a person having his hand cut off, then when we attempt to form pictures of our external "I"s grabbing someone's purse, we will recall a picture our external "I"s having our hand cut off and the second set of neuronic impacts will prevent us from forming pictures that will allow us to act in response to the first set of neuronic impacts, pictures of ourselves possessing what we don't have, and we will stop forming pictures of our external "I"s engaged in the acts we would need to take to posses what we don't have, the acts won't occur and we will end up receiving no neuronic impacts.

The protection of the individual's space and property, the individual's inner concentric circles of recall, is absolutely necessary for society to come together. This protection is accomplished by establishing a ubiquitous "I" that informs individuals how to behave by creating a connection between the very real pain of physical punishment and violations of the prohibitions that define Golden Rule Behavior.

We are driven to come together in societies because we can not face the holes that appear in our recall when we can create a picture of reality in recall when reality is not present and because numbers provide us with food, shelter and safety with fewer neuronic impacts than obtaining food, shelter and safety on our own would produce.

But gathering in societies presents a whole new set of neuronic impacts, protecting the possessions that occupy the inner concentric circles of our recall and coveting the possessions occupying the inner concentric circles of the recall of others.

Society has to minimize the neuronic impacts its members experience because a society that allows more neuronic impacts than would occur were the individual on his own would soon be abandoned by its members and cease to be.

There is, however, a hierarchy of neuronic impacts, of pain, that drives us to form and maintain society. Recall generated by the physical necessity arising from a lack of food is at the top of the hierarchy of neuronic impacts that drive us to act in physical reality.

When there isn't enough food, society can agree that societal efforts should be directed toward obtaining more food.

What happens when the need for food encounters society's prohibitions against violations of Golden Rule Behavior?

As we saw when our little miscreant burned down the community storehouse, empty stomachs can combine to accomplish a common goal. Hunger pangs produce common recall, food, and when a group of people have the same recall, they can organize their external "I"s around actions that will accomplish a common goal, the goal of obtaining food. If the only available food belongs to another group that occupies a wider concentric circle in our recall than our own group, and the only way to get the food to satisfy our hunger pains is to make mincemeat out of the people that make up the other group, then that is what we are going to do.

There will, most certainly, be members of our group that don't want to have anything to do with the use of force to take another's food, which is the taking of the possessions of another, because forming a picture of their external "I"s taking the possessions of another would produce neuronic impacts based on the societal programming incorporated into the ubiquitous "I" informed by Golden Rule Behavior.

In fact, to maintain the ubiquitous "I" that holds the fabric of society together, it is important that as few people as possible be required to violate the prohibitions that define Golden Rule Behavior and as many people as possible believe that any violations that come to light are justified.

Anytime we allow others to produce our recall for us, we have abdicated the responsibility to produce that recall for ourselves.

If we abdicate our responsibility to produce recall about force and motion, we create an authority in others to produce that recall for us. If we abdicate our responsibility to produce recall about the source of our existence, we create an authority to produce that recall for us. If we abdicate our responsibility to produce recall that would control our actions, we create an authority in others to produce that recall for us.

In the first two instances, we have created mystical and spiritual authorities, and in the latter case, we have created civil authority.

When the need for food drives society to utilize the first authority, the technology of war, to transcend the latter two authorities, the spiritual and civil requirement for Golden Rule Behavior, even when the civil authorities come to us and say: "We absolve you from our programming, forget the ubiquitous 'I' for now, you're exempted from the dictates of an eye for an eye, you can go out and maim and kill until everybody gets their bellies full!," we will still feel the neuronic impacts from engaging in acts that violate societal behavior because forming pictures of ourselves doing something the ubiquitous "I" has been programmed not to do creates an unavoidable conflict that produces pain.

Even if we could convince ourselves that the suspension of punishment by the civil authorities freed us from the dictates of the ubiquitous "I" and thus were able to eliminate our neuronic impacts from this source, if we have been programmed by the spiritual authorities that represent our gods to fear hell and eternal damnation for violations of Golden Rule Behavior, we will still face the pain of neuronic impacts from that source.

If we answer the civil authorities that they cannot absolve us from religious punishment because they don't administer it, we might still receive absolution from the religious authorities, who could claim that starving the infidels preserves the faith and that taking their food is just another way of glorifying our maker.

But once we have been programmed by the dictates of the ubiquitous "I" informed by Golden Rule Behavior, we cannot ourselves escape the neuronic impacts the ubiquitous "I" is designed to create

Moral and civil considerations aside, however, one fact remains: Either the members of society organize themselves to obtain the needed food no matter what, or everybody in society ceases to exist.

Going back to thee and me and a one-man life raft, there is no question of the outcome. One of us is going to survive, the other isn't, and the one that survives is the one that takes from the one that doesn't!

When society is prospering, when its resources are rising when compared to its population and the needs and wants of that population, the nine percent can provide for the ninety with minimal conflict and the remaining one percent can take the cream or the leavings as they scramble to stay out of jail.

The nine percent receive ample rewards and with the ninety percent fat, dumb and happy, the rewards go unquestioned.

But when the population outstrips the available resources, when the question of who scores the winning touchdown is replaced with the question of who scores the last scrap of food, the rewards of the nine become pain because it must itself direct the ninety percent to participate in or condone acts that violate Golden Rule Behavior while attempting to preserve that behavior in society as a whole.

The nine percent may no longer have intellectual "I"s dictated by a ubiquitous "I" informed by Golden Rule Behavior because prosperity has replaced that ubiquitous "I" with one informed by Exalted Empathy, the need to help those less fortunate than themselves, but the members of the nine percent are still forced to maintain the appearance of compliance with Golden Rule Behavior.

An intellectual "I" informed by a ubiquitous "I" that requires that we help those less fortunate than ourselves allows unlimited behavior by leaving open the definition of those less fortunate than ourselves. Driven by Exalted Empathy, we can easily reconcile the slaughter of millions by defining those less fortunate as a world that is unsafe without democracy or as a world straining to release the chains of the capitalist warmonger.

However, even though the slaughter of millions will not produce neuronic impacts in those whose intellectual "I"s are informed by a ubiquitous "I" that dictates Exalted Empathy, society still has to maintain Golden Rule Behavior because Golden Rule Behavior is the glue that holds society together. The nine percent enlist those informed by Golden Rule Behavior to violate Golden Rule Behavior by reprogramming the ninety percent, taking advantage of the fact that we only have one mind and thus can only hold one picture of reality, and one intellectual "I" in recall at any one time.

Although a percentage of society will always refuse to violate Golden Rule Behavior because they can not shake the original programming, the vast majority of the ninety percent will be just as susceptible to the reprogramming as they were to the original programming. They will readily respond to the imperative to fight or be punished, and will join the rank and file of the machinery developed to carry out the taking, the violations of Golden Rule Behavior that will lead to full bellies for all.

In situations involving the protection or expansion of society's basic needs, all members of society become those at the center of each member's inner concentric circle of recall, a circle that expands outward to encompass the society as a whole, the society organizing itself to do the taking, as opposed to others, those outside the circle, those not dear to recall who are therefore capable of being demonized, characterized as beasts and devils, those whose possessions are going to be taken.

Because the nine percent are doing the programming and because Exalted Empathy requires acts as opposed to prohibitions against acting, the ninety percent are programmed with a new ubiquitous "I" that dictates that they concentrate on how to act rather than on how not to act.

This shift from prohibiting acts to requiring acts arises because a successful taking requires awareness, the division between the nine and the ninety is one of awareness and the nine percent, those whose ubiquitous "I" prescribes acts, are the aware.

The ubiquitous "I" informed by Exalted Empathy requires acts rather than prohibitions against acting because it requires acts to raise those less fortunate. Without acts, those less fortunate will remain less fortunate.

Individuals driven by a ubiquitous "I" informed by Exalted Empathy are driven to act, driven to improve the lot of those they considers less fortunate, and their Exalted Empathy is concerned with prescribing rather than proscribing behavior. In a society whose leaders respond to a ubiquitous "I" informed by Exalted Empathy, the laws are not so much concerned with punishment for violations of Golden Rule Behavior as with punishments for failure to act in certain ways.

Thus, when the nine percent reprogram the ubiquitous "I" that controls the behavior of the ninety percent in order that the ninety percent may participate in the necessary acts that violate Golden Rule Behavior without receiving the pain of neuronic impacts, the programming overwrites the requirement that the ninety percent refrain from acting in a certain way and dictates that they perform those acts necessary to have a successful outcome in the taking which, to disguise the nature of the activity, is always defined as defensive to reflect the need to act.

Saving tin foil and rubber bands to defend the homeland become positive programming, acts that occupy the mind and obscure the nature of the taking even though there is no recycling and thus the acts have no effect on the outcome.

Because we only have a single intellectual "I" in recall at any one time, the intellectual "I" informed by a ubiquitous "I" that is prescribing acts eliminates the ubiquitous "I" that proscribes acts and the ninety percent sacrifice themselves to the effort involved in a successful taking.

The old ubiquitous "I" has been suspended for God and Country. Moral equivocation is not permitted. Violations of Golden Rule Behavior attract medals and parades with the greater the violations, the bigger the parades.

Members of the ninety percent that aspire to and are competent in policy making jobs leave the ninety percent and join the nine. The rest remain, merely seeking to remain free of neuronic impacts, proscribing or prescribing their behavior as dictated by society in exchange for society's benefits.

The nine percent of society directing the taking, on the other hand, have to act with a clear picture, a lucid comprehension, a total awareness that successful operations involve conscious violations of Golden Rule Behavior. They are faced with a constant conflict between reality and the need to produce recall that obscures the actual nature of reality, of the taking, because allowing reality to intrude might burst the bubble that temporarily prevents the recall by the ninety percent of the requirement to observe Golden Rule Behavior.

The nine percent endure the pain of these neuronic impacts as the necessary anguish that results from their having to take actions that in normal times they would never contemplate taking.

For the benefit of the ninety percent, the nine percent can reference moral goals to assuage their neuronic impacts, either a moral commitment to protect the right to private property that is at the basis of the social contract or a moral commitment to a socialistic society that transcends any basic moral considerations dealing with private property and thus Golden Rule Behavior. These rationalizations allow them in turn to easily redirect the gaze of the ninety percent away from violations of Golden Rule Behavior, remove restraints on those actions necessary to accomplish the goal of the conflict, the taking of another's property and obscure the consequences of their actions by claiming that they are helping those less fortunate than themselves.

Which leaves the one percent, the small group that have escaped ubiquitous "I" programming altogether.

The one percent, not subject to the societal programming against violations of Golden Rule Behavior, are capable of forming the clearest pictures of the recall necessary to accomplish the taking and, as a result, easily rise to positions of leadership.

Obviously, when a society is prosperous, the recall of the ninety percent predominates because the ninety percent accounts for ninety percent of the commerce. The recall of the ninety percent, more in accord with the prosperous nine percent, deals with leisure and the arts and therefore commerce is organized around satisfying wants associated with sports and movies, recreation and dalliances.

However, if a society is threatened internally by physical wants or externally by the physical wants of other societies, the importance of the one percent who have no compunction about violating Golden Rule Behavior, rises accordingly.

The business of taking what we need involves sacrifices up to and including the ultimate sacrifice, the sacrifice of existence and thus it is not a pleasant affair. The aftermath is even less pleasant because we have to live with our acts after our needs have been satisfied. We have to encase our acts in glory, in marching bands and monuments in celebration of the glorious victories so that our recall can be fuzzed over and replaced and our neuronic impacts diminished and eliminated.

When the taking is over, the ninety percent return to acting in accordance with the dictates of Golden Rule Behavior, their memories of the conflict but a dream stored at current levels that are not assessable by the intellectual "I" whose thoughts are procured by Golden Rule Behavior.

Ninety percent of the members of society live their day to day lives praying they won't be called to sacrifice in their lifetimes, and the remaining ten percent, aware to one degree or another, and willing to accept the burden of that awareness, the neuronic impacts that result from engaging in acts prohibited by society even where those acts are necessary to preserve society, pretty much direct the affairs of the society.

There is a ruling class, and the existence of the ruling class benefits the other ninety percent of society by holding it together so that Golden Rule Behavior can produce a degree of consistency in the lives of the entire society.

We do find descriptions from the logs of early Pacific voyages describing societies that fought constantly over physical necessities. These societies, isolated on islands whose limited resources were easily affected by changing weather patterns, existed in a perpetual state of warfare. The intensity of the fighting waxed and waned with the availability of the resources, the defeated becoming food for the victors.

Without pointing out that these societies may well be the remnants of a larger society that was inundated and whose cities can be found under tens of feet of water throughout the Pacific from Tonga to Japan, rather than primitive societies that never achieved civilization, this is not the template for slaughter we have grown accustomed to on this planet.

The necessities of trade, of commerce, the exploitation of the farming and mineral resources of the Earth and the labor of others have driven our minds to produce a different sort of template, a template produced not by the neuronic impacts created by hunger, but by the neuronic impacts created by producing recall of theoretical possessions.

The drive to benefit from the prosperity technology produces creates an entirely different relationship between the nine percent that direct the affairs of society and the ninety percent that demand the fruits of that direction than exists when the basic purpose of society is to provide food, shelter and safety. Because the wants that recall can produce are unlimited, and can be produced by everyone anywhere as soon as awareness is created of the existence of the goods and services that give rise to those wants, competition for prosperity replaces the basic competition for food as soon as our wants exceed our basic physical needs.

When we are marching out to fill our bellies, we are dealing with physical subjugation. When we are satisfying our myriad wants for flat hats and spectator sports, we are dealing with commercial exploitation.

Competition for prosperity is based on the operation of the same mind that brings individuals together into a society. We see our external "I"s having possessions we don't have in reality and, when we obtain those possessions, we become accustomed to possessions the loss of which would put a hole in our recall.

When we are not in competition for food and shelter, when we have utilized our leisure time to produce a technology that produces a rising prosperity, then the nine percent whose ubiquitous "I" is informed by Exalted Empathy is free to concern itself with raising the level of those less fortunate, which is the remaining ninety percent. The benefit of technology, prosperity, spreads rapidly to all members of the society because as long as one member of society does not benefit equally from the fruits of technology, there is someone less fortunate whose level can be raised.

However, with the fruits of technology expanding outward from the prosperous to the less prosperous, the prosperity of the society as a whole continually rises, increasing the number of those less fortunate.

The nine percent, driven by Exalted Empathy to raise the level of those less fortunate, have to find the resources to expand the prosperity to those less fortunate somewhere. That somewhere, on this particular planet which has been fractured into a multiplicity of societies, is elsewhere.

A society that succeeds in using technology to establish prosperity also uses that technology to take the resources of other societies in order to maintain and expand the prosperity throughout the society.

Thus, even in the absence of war, the nine percent, and to a certain extent, the one percent, must engage in activities that violate Golden Rule Behavior to maintain the prosperity of the ninety percent of society whose ubiquitous "I" is informed by the need for Golden Rule Behavior.

The division of ninety, nine and one has thus become a continuing division of awareness in which the nine percent are constantly required to consciously violate Golden Rule Behavior to provide for the prosperity of society as a whole while the ninety percent of society informed by Golden Rule Behavior are completely unaware that it takes violations of Golden Rule Behavior to provide for the prosperity that has become a part of the inner concentric circles of their recall.

The ninety percent are not aware by design because an awareness that their comforts were the result of the discomforts of others would produce neuronic impacts, pain, on multiple levels, first by causing the ninety percent to realize that their comfort depends on violations of the same Golden Rule Behavior that informs the ubiquitous "I, standards of conduct which they have been taught all their lives and which are a part of their self, and second by the fear of losing the comforts that have become part of the inner concentric circles of their recall.

Now we really have a problem with hypocrisy, the conflict of society's actions when compared with the actions against which society programs its members. Private property rights are at the basis of society, but to obtain prosperity, a society has to consistently and on a continuing basis violate the private property rights of members of other societies.

It's a conundrum solved by realizing that acts are just the movement of matter in reality while the recall of acts is defined by the neuronic impacts that recall of the acts produces, neuronic impacts that define morality.

Society evolves to satisfy the needs of its members and its existence rests on the enforcement of Golden Rule Behavior.

But possession turns wants into needs and with no limitation on the resulting needs, society can no longer satisfy the needs of its members.

However, providing for the needs of its members is the reason society exists, so society has to satisfy those needs by taking from other societies. Because other societies resist the taking, a segment of society has to continually violate the rules of behavior that hold the society together.

When the growth of a society's wants moves it past military aggression where the violations of Golden Rule Behavior are performed outside the recall of the ninety percent, to economic exploitation, invisible aggression where prosperity and its consumption is always at the expense of others, then the continuing violations of Golden Rule Behavior become, like the myriad unsatisfied wants prosperity produces, background noise that permeates societal interactions.

Persistent economic exploitation is no different from two intellectual "I"s simultaneously forming pictures of their external "I"s reaching for the same piece of fruit.

There is a conflict.

Only one is going to get the fruit.

In the competition for world resources, in a world where those resources are dwindling and will vanish, only one society is going to eat the fruit.

But for that society to exist, it members must be programmed with Golden Rule Behavior.

The ninety percent of societal members programmed to follow Golden Rule Behavior must be protected from the fact that the fruit they are driven by neuronic impacts to posses is sourced in violations of Golden Rule Behavior.

It's as simple as that!

The one percent of society's members that have allegiance neither to Golden Rule Behavior nor Exalted Empathy because they are impervious to it, they were protected from being inculcated with it, they are protected from the consequences of their acts, they are from outside the society, or their Golden Rule Behavior is shaped by different considerations, join the nine percent in organizing and directing the continuing activities that result in the successful elimination of effective competition against obtaining the resources demanded by the other ninety percent. This group organizes itself around the military needed to protect society and the commerce that society demands.

In our world, the today of this planet, the external "I" that takes the fruit is the external "I" with the biggest club!

The activities and the extensive planning for the activities necessary to preserve and expand the satisfaction of society's needs have to be carried out without the awareness of the ninety percent of the society that are the direct beneficiaries of the activities because otherwise those beneficiaries would be subject to neuronic impacts which would drive some of the members to attack the society that was benefiting them, and if enough of the members became aware of the inconsistency between programming and acts, and received a sufficient level of neuronic impacts as a result of being aware of the hypocrisy, they might well attack and destroy the society or destroy it by drifting off, abandoning it because they would experience a lower level of neuronic impacts elsewhere.

If we had evolved in a normal fashion, without being splintered asunder by a planet-wide catastrophe, the problems involved in unifying consumption around available resources would have washed themselves out with millions of tiny, isolated conflicts as groups gained cohesion or eliminated competitors around the dwindling resources.

Instead, the planet was fractured into dozens of groups that first organized themselves around geographical areas that provided resources for survival and the reemergence of society, and then those groups, as populations increased, produced technology that created needs and expanded the beneficiaries of existing needs. With the escalating needs produced by technology, the technology had to be directed to establishing and maintaining trade dominance.

Because of the absolute importance of trade to prosperity, the need to satisfy unlimited wants, the technology that developed was technology that was useful in trade, either to improve its efficiency, or more importantly, to protect it from competition.

Because the only way to protect trade from competition is conflict, we devoted our efforts to developing technology that improved our methods of killing each other rather than in technology that improved our methods of extending our range of survivability in physical reality. Because our recall has been focused entirely on methods of resolving conflicts by eliminating those conflicts, the recall we created to explain how things work in reality became secondary to making those things work. Instead of asking questions about the nature of the force that makes objects move when they are dropped, we spent our time creating recall dealing with how we could overcome that force, how we could devise methods to hurl bombs further and transport them faster. Instead of asking questions about the process of burning, the nature of energy, the source of force, we spent our time creating recall dealing with how we could make bigger and more destructive explosions.

Without recall explaining the nature of the force that holds us to the surface of the Earth or how the energy that drives motion in the universe is created, travels and affects matter, we have no chance of extending our range of survivability in physical reality, and the technology that we do happen upon through trial and error experimentation is incapable of producing the prosperity that would eliminate the incessant conflicts to which happenstance has made us heir.

Because the people that control society are organized around trade and trade represents wealth, they benefit from the prosperity. The miller always has the freshest grains, the well keeper the cleanest water, the tiller of vines the sweetest wine. Those that stand between society and its potential destruction and enslavement by competing interests are heir to benefits that are the emoluments of their position, and not the result of private gain.

However, the job of managing a society's business with respect to competing systems is not the desirable job that it might appear. The trade routes, the paths of commerce become institutions that have to deliver the wants of society or suffer the wrath of the anger unfulfilled wants produces. These institutions organize the production of wealth around the financial interests the wealth creates and the leaders of the institutions become slaves to the dictates of the financial interests.

The financial interests are not money, or gold bullion or credit, which are themselves merely processes created to conduct effective trade.

The financial interests are the successful creation of the overall system, a suprasocietal structure whose authority is greater than the authority dealing with behavior that the society creates so that its members can safely interact with one another with minimal damage to the society. The British Empire fell to its inability to establish such a suprasocietal structure that organized the production of wealth around financial interests, limiting itself to an Old Boy's Club system in which disparate clubs represented different financial interests.

The globally oriented society that is the United States has attempted to organize in a manner that will lead to the reconsolidation of the Earth's fractured societies.

While John D. Rockefeller Senior is painted as a monopolist and robber baron, his business philosophy is at the core of attempts extending over the course of the twentieth century to produce institutions that organize the products of wealth around the financial interests the wealth produces in order to unify the diverse societies of the world into a single society.

This philosophy is composed of four basic principles.

The Senior Rockefeller understood the first principle instinctively, although his many detractors fail to perceive it to this day.

Trade requires customers, and the ideal trade is carried out at a price that makes customers of everyone.

In his youth, during the wild frenzy of the oil discoveries, the Senior Rockefeller could clearly see demand producing price increases which, attracting producers, caused gluts. The gluts would then reduce prices to the point that producers would go bankrupt. Bankruptcies eliminated supply, once again creating a demand that raised prices to attract producers.

Such a process of boom and bust created an inefficient delivery of product raising the overall cost of product to customers who need a consistent supply at the lowest possible price.

Prosperity is based on the continued movement of goods and services to the source of the demand.

Organizing a system that produced the efficient delivery of product on a consistent basis, the Senior Rockefeller was excoriated as the embodiment of greed. However, his Standard Oil Trust was actually a slave to the efficient delivery system that resulted and thus to its customers. Even the smallest price increase shocked the system, reducing consumption, while the smallest efficiency, producing barrel staves without overlaps, produced an engineered increase in consumption.

The only way to expand trade, then, became the drive for efficiency, accomplished by excellence, rather than the imputed profit, which is actually the feature of the system that objectively determines the optimal allocation of capital.

The resulting consumer driven efficiency has taken over the world in today's market driven economy.

While the United States dominates world trade, the Senior Rockefeller's second innovation, the Trust System, spread ownership of the trade operations to those capable of improving it.

Under the system, which replaced all systems of class and caste, all contributors become a part of the financial interests driving the system. The result has been to extend what would normally have been a societally driven grouping of financial interests into a grouping of interests from many societies with a common interest in preserving and expanding world trade.

The openness of the system which allows all contributors ownership interest, created the third principle established by the Senior Rockefeller, a principle that is in full operation today, that ingenuity and enterprise no matter what the source are equal to or better than a money stake to buy into the system.

This principle opens the system to all on the basis of excellence alone.

Essentially, these three principles, incorporated into the successful business philosophy that drives the emerging world market economy basically structured the nine percent at the helm of society in a way that creates a revolving door which allows capital and technological ingenuity continued entrance and the failure to contribute a rapid exit in order to open the system to members of all societies to expand a diverse society to consolidate a fractured world.

This consolidation leads to the fourth principle, a principle established by the war between the states, the Civil War, the defining conflict for the Senior Rockefeller as a young man. The Civil War codified the principle that fractured societies, once solidified, shall never again be fractured.

The incredibly large conflicts that have occurred in the twentieth century are merely the formulation of a successful system that will eliminate the competing systems that grew out of the initial fracturing of the unified society that would normally have evolved on this particular planet and will, by its success, eliminate the problem inherent in the resulting societies, that to survive they have to engage in violations of the Golden Rule Behavior that holds them together, and leave a system driven by the demand of societal members for the efficient servicing of their needs and thus a system driven by excellence.

That appears to be the system that is evolving to overcome the obstacles to which we are unwitting heirs.

Those that attempt, through ignorance of the system, or pure stupidity, to convert the flow of public benefits to private interests, will be destroyed by the system, and those outside the system that attempt to oppose it will merely be destroyed.

However, that doesn't mean the system will succeed.

The system results from behavior dictated by the operation of the mind and it can collapse as a result of behavior dictated by the operation of the mind.

12. CONSUMED BY CHARITABLE IMPERATIVES

One of the beneficial by-products of forming together into societies is the exercise we get in withstanding the pain of current neuronic impacts. We endure them because we know that if we act in response to them, we will receive even worse neuronic impacts in the future.

Socialization teaches us how to hold our temper.

Temper is what we call controlling the pain produced by neuronic impacts. When we feel pain, we lash out at the source of the pain because we physically need to get rid of the pain. Because the source of the pain is the unwanted electrical flows in our bodies, and because muscle movement dissipates the electrons that make up the electric flows, we attempt to relieve our pain by yelling, flailing our fists, kicking and throwing things which all work to dissipate the unwanted flows by moving our muscles.

Holding our temper means freezing our muscles against the reflexive actions the unwanted electrical flows create. It also involves putting a damper on the pictures of mayhem the feedback from these neuronic impacts recall. One way to get rid of the pictures of mayhem is to use the feedback to generate unrelated pictures. Like some would-be Casanova trying to win an endurance contest by mentally reciting the math tables, we can count from one to ten while the black cloud dissipates from above our head.

We can't respond to the provocations in physical reality if we don't have pictures in recall of ourselves responding to those provocations.

We see people lose their tempers when we cut them off in a car, tease them about a physical characteristic or contradict their basic beliefs, saying their god is false.

When we are being assaulted, when someone or something is preventing our free movement in physical reality by cutting us off in a car, creating a picture of reality that doesn't exist in our recall, or is producing a picture of our external "I"s that isn't compatible with the intellectual "I"s in our recall by belittling our size or shape, or is messing with our ubiquitous "I", the repository of societally programmed beliefs, by assaulting our gods, an assault so basic that it might send us off to the far corners of the Earth to smite the infidel, we are subject to neuronic impacts that are actual pain.

We hurt.

Our composure is threatened by this pain, and if we give into the pain, if we allow ourselves to form the pictures that would produce actions appropriate to the assault, we might just ram the other person with our car, punch him in the nose or burn him on a big bonfire.

Holding our composure against the onslaught of unwanted neuronic impacts is to temper our behavior.

Behavior is our reaction to the pain of neuronic impacts and societally appropriate behavior is the constraints we impose on ourselves to comply with the societal dictates of the ubiquitous "I" informed by Golden Rule Behavior.

The ubiquitous "I" informed by Golden Rule Behavior is filled with prohibitions against just the sort of behavior that would result if we allowed our recall to produce pictures of our external "I"s performing the acts we would like to perform in response to the provocations that produce the neuronic impacts, acts which would momentarily make us feel good if we performed them.

The reason that we temper our behavior when it comes to societal laws is that we know, because of serial recall, that performing acts in violation of the law will result in punishment.

The prospect of punishment prevents us from performing the acts.

But what happens when our responses are not covered by the law and do not carry punishment? We lose our temper all the time. We shout, throw things, bang our shoe on a desk, get up, walk out, slam the door behind us and generally behave like unschooled children.

It's a great feeling!

Losing our temper allows us to form a picture of our external "I"s doing something that agrees with our recall at the same time that it gives our muscles a way to dissipate the unwanted electrical energy produced by the neuronic impacts, relieving our minds of having to deal with the feedback and our bodies of having to suffer the pain of neuronic impacts.

Sometimes losing our temper is irresistible!

Although ceaseless in their efforts, there is no way civil authorities can pass and enforce enough laws to control all undesirable behavior or dictate all desirable behavior. As a result, the ubiquitous "I", with a basic purpose of eliminating neuronic impacts, has an underlying principle that we should all get along with one another.

Therefore, after we have lost our temper, after we have committed acts in reality out of the simple pleasure of giving in to the need to match reality with recall to relieve ourselves of our pain, after we have laid down our tracks in physical reality, we are left with a picture in our recall of our external "I"s out of control which doesn't match the primary picture of our external "I"s dictated by the ubiquitous "I", a picture of our external "I"s calm and in control.

Every time we recall our external "I"s acting in a manner that opposes the dictates of the ubiquitous "I" that we should all get along with one another, we get neuronic impacts.

When we give in to our temper, when we lose control of ourselves in an effort to rid ourselves of the passing pain of momentary neuronic impacts, we create recall that gives us neuronic impacts for the rest of our lives!

How bad these neuronic impacts are depends on the circumstances that caused us to lose our temper and the extent to which we responded to those circumstances, what produced our loss of temper and how great our loss of temper was.

When we have lost our temper and feel that the resulting acts are justified, we will never receive neuronic impacts. However, if those within our inner concentric circles of recall demand decorum, if we are aware that our acts have disturbed the peaceful interrelationships of those around us, then to the extent that our acts have disturbed the peace, we have to minimize the recall that produces the neuronic impacts that result when we recall our loss of temper. To do this, we have to atone for our loss of temper and the acts that resulted from that loss.

We have to find who we directed our wrath at and apologize.

This might produce a picture of our external "I"s that conflicts with our intellectual "I"s to such an extent that we can't form a picture of ourselves apologizing. If we can't form a picture of ourselves apologizing and therefore can not apologize, we might just have to live with the neuronic impacts produced by recalling the acts. This could put us in the same position as a rape victim who becomes promiscuous, causing us to repeat the act to match the picture of the violation, turning us from societal lambs into mad, bad, dangerous lads.

However, if we can bring ourselves to atone for our acts, we produce pictures of our external "I"s that are totally in agreement with the ubiquitous "I", which, generated by the interactions among the members that make up society, has at its basis the dictate that we should all get along with one another.

Things which are so basic to our recall that we take them as unquestioned reality reside in the ubiquitous "I". This is where society programs its authority, where religious beliefs, concepts of God and morality, our picture of where we came from and how people should behave, reside.

When the infidel appears in our recall profaning our god, either because we have witnessed him doing so in person or, more likely, because we have had a picture painted for us in our recall of him doing so, the conflict goes directly to our essence, to our core beliefs, to the ubiquitous "I" installed from birth and the resulting rage is far greater than the response to neuronic impacts that occurs when we get thrown into a mud puddle.

On the other hand, the absence of neuronic impacts does drive behavior, just as being tired drives us to sit down. We feel a distinct pleasure at having pain removed, and we feel even more pleasure when our external "I"s can do things that exactly match recall. The elation at hitting a home run at the bottom of the ninth, seventh game of the World Series, bases loaded, down three, is almost too much to bear. We high five, jump up and down, shout with glee, grab our teammates, generally go crazy.

What we are doing is matching in reality a recall that we have spent so many daydreams and night wishes recreating that we have placed the picture in the ubiquitous "I". The image of the individual as hero is as old as Alexander marching out to conquer the world and as persistent as David bringing Goliath down in the desert.

We have in the ubiquitous "I" images of the ideal, how things should be if things were absolutely as they should be, and when those things are recreated in reality, we are overcome with ecstasy or whatever rising emotion we haven't bred out of ourselves in order to preserve the image of our external "I"s in the face of mores against emoting.

Just as our subsystems are subjected to the unwanted flows of electricity when our minds stop operating as a result of recall and reality disagreeing, when reality attempts to match the idealistic behavior embodied in the ubiquitous "I", we have a sort of epiphany in which the mind pauses. When we are in a quiet room listening to the ticking of a clock, we are recalling static reality. There is no difference between recall and reality, and no comprehension. When we are matching reality with ideal recall, we are producing comprehension, but we don't understand what that comprehension is. Our minds leak some electricity as a result, much of it affecting the contiguous facial muscles and thus producing uniformity of expression in response to social situations, but a lot more of it being withdrawn by our sinuses and tear ducts, and we associate the effect on our subsystems as pleasurable (or embarrassing if it conflicts with a macho external "I").

Movies take advantage of this characteristic by pulling on our heartstrings, the events on celluloid, simulating reality, gradually approaching agreement with a societal ideal. No matter how much we see resolved love or victory over the implacable and evil enemy coming, we still can't avoid our response, our emotional elevation, because the response is simply the result of how the mind operates.

When we apologize, we have produced a recall about the incident in which we lost our temper that overwrites the recall of the incident. In addition, we have matched our action in reality with the societal ideal. Having foreknowledge that a feeling of exaltation will result is certainly an incentive to apologize, the good feelings that will result from having recall that agrees with the societal ideal being better than the feelings resulting from recall of our external "I"s engaging in iffy, even prohibited, conduct.

Lover's arguments beget the bliss of making up!

When we walk down the street and someone less fortunate than ourselves comes up to us with a stained Styrofoam coffee cup in an outstretched hand, we reach into our pocket or purse, take out some change and plop it in the cup. The mind drives this transaction in the following manner:

We are walking down the street in response to our recall forming pictures of our external "I"s walking down the street.

We are presented with a picture of someone less fortunate than ourselves, a sort of, eat your food, children are starving in Panglonia sort of recall.

We form a picture of our external "I"s out on the street in the cold with no place to go and nothing to eat.

We receive neuronic impacts which get our attention and which produce a picture of our external "I"s taking some coins out of our pocket or purse and dropping them in the cup.

We take some coins out of our pocket or purse and drop then in the cup.

We walk on, our recall now containing a picture of our external "I"s doing something that accords with the societal ideal and we feel good about ourselves.

We have given something back.

We are a good person!

The treatment that our external "I"s get in physical reality determines to a large extent the nature of our intellectual "I"s. The difference between the ubiquitous "I" and our intellectual "I" is the recall that we can change our intellectual "I"s. The standard of conduct dictated by the ubiquitous "I" is a standard of conduct that our external "I"s have to live up to, and our intellectual "I"s are the "self" that makes the choices whether to be good or bad as measured against the standard of the ubiquitous "I".

It is this match, the agreement of our behavior with societal expectations, that gives our lives meaning.

But our "self", our intellectual "I"s are many different "selfs." We have an intellectual "I" when we go to work, we have another one when we romance our spouse, still another one when we play with the kids (and still another unexpected one when we play with the grandkids), we have one for when we are sick, and all sorts of "selfs" for when we dream, when the current that operates our minds, in a condition opposite to the raised current level of sexual arousal, is so low that it picks up bits and pieces of recall in our neuronic storage bins and crafts them into exotic configurations that, at the normal current levels of everyday movement, are not recallable, but merely distant memories of the implausibly possible.

What we end up with is a slightly unstable "self" sandwiched between our external "I" which gets beaten up and battered day in and day out as we move through physical reality, and the ubiquitous "I" which sits behind our eyes between our ears in uncompromising judgment.

When our intellectual "I"s fade a little, it becomes harder to maintain pictures of our external "I"s opposing physical reality. If the boss says crawl, we will probably crawl.

However, if our intellectual "I"s are in pretty good shape, are stable, then when the boss says crawl, our intellectual "I"s might well be strong enough to form a picture of our external "I"s throwing the old bear the bird.

How well we are able to maintain the clarity of our intellectual "I"s depends on how well we are able to maintain pictures of our external "I"s engaging in acts which agree with our intellectual "I"s as informed by the ubiquitous "I" in the face of opposition from the temptations and denigrations of those around us.

Because of the instability of our intellectual "I"s and because we look for acceptance from those around us, those occupying our inner concentric circles of recall, agreement with those in our inner concentric circles of recall tends to produce a consensus reality that can completely replace the ubiquitous "I" that would normally inform our actions.

We occupy, after all, the center of a group of concentric circles made up of the recall containing the events that occur around us together with the people that make up those events. The people making up the events that occupy the closer concentric circles of our recall make up a larger portion of our recall and thus are included in a larger portion of our intellectual "I"s than the people further from the center.

As a result, the people in the inner concentric circles, the people closer to our "self" appear more in our recall.

When everyone in the circles in which we operate agree with us and when we agree with everyone who occupy the circles in which we operate, then we operate on the basis of a consensus recall. Because we are all operating on the basis of the same recall, we are operating in furtherance of a consensus reality and we make up a consensual coterie.

Because we operate in furtherance of the pictures we form in our recall and because consensus reality is recall, we tend to look to our consensual coterie for the approval or disapproval of our actions before we examine how those acts might be informed by the ubiquitous "I".

This is the process that evolves the ubiquitous "I"!

Consensual coteries form at every level and in every segment of society from bridge clubs and associations of particle physicists, through local lodges and the world of art critics, to the Office of the President and the Queen's Bedchamber. Manufacturing their own realities that can temporarily replace the ubiquitous "I", consensual coteries can have far reaching consequences when they form in isolation at the top of corporations, in the upper echelons of military groups, especially if they are revolutionary groups, and in political operations which, accustomed to creating pictures of reality that can never exist in reality, are particularly prone to the loss of perspective that results from the isolation consensual coteries create.

Consensual coteries evolve because we look to those in our recall, in the inner concentric circles surrounding our intellectual "I"s for the support that is necessary to form the pictures of our external "I"s effectively acting in physical reality. Our intellectual "I" is not as stable as the ubiquitous "I", which is programmed to an objective standard, and because intellectual "I"s are interchangeable in response to changing physical reality, where we are, what we are doing and who we are doing it with, one or the other of our intellectual "I"s is going to permit our external "I"s the pleasures society seeks to deny us regardless of the ubiquitous "I".

Temptation sends our regular intellectual "I"s, and along with them, the ubiquitous "I", into hibernation. We continually violate societal prohibitions and we continually strike out against others with inappropriate acts we perceive as justified at the time.

Our interactions with others in reality, either personally, professionally, or sexually, taken sober or under the influence, constantly result in violations of the behavior dictated by the ubiquitous "I", what we consider to be our regular intellectual "I", and even the limits we set ourselves for permissible violations of societal prohibitions.

In addition, questions of interpretation constantly shade the meaning of societal prohibitions, what our regular intellectual "I"s permit, even who we are.

We are always faced with the question of whether our acts were or are proper!

To find the answer to this constant question, we look for approval from those around us. We all begin to reflect each other's recall and everybody's shared reality becomes the reality of the consensual coterie.

Consensual coteries, regardless of their interests, cluster around wealth, either in an effort to obtain it or in an effort to protect it against those attempting to obtain it. The nine percent that is closest to a society's prosperity is made up of consensual coteries containing people who are better educated, possess more of the material goods provided by trade, and, because they have traveled, have broader horizons. They are more aware of how the world operates, or to be more precise, they are aware that there is more than one way to operate a world, that societies have different values, different prohibitions and different ways to punish transgressions.

As a result, the reality of consensual coteries can lead to the establishment of empires and the ruination of nations depending on how closely the reality of a particular consensual coterie matches physical reality.

How we stabilize our intellectual "I"s against the uncertainties of acting in physical reality with the pictures of reality produced by consensual coteries determines how we act because without a stable intellectual "I", without the capability of forming a solid picture of our external "I"s acting in physical reality, we simply can not act.

This doesn't mean that there aren't some people for whom the ubiquitous "I" is so controlling that it never permits a variation of the intellectual "I", or for whom the intellectual "I" is the ubiquitous "I" so that acts never have to be questioned. It simply means that the vast majority of us need some way to maintain our intellectual "I"s with a degree of stability. To bolster that stability when our external "I"s have been pummeled in physical reality, to bolster our confidence in the appropriateness of our behavior, we look at how others in our consensual coterie view our behavior.

Another way of bolstering our confidence in the appropriateness of our behavior, to stabilize our intellectual "I"s when our external "I"s are getting buffeted about, is to build up a storehouse of recall that shows us being good people.

Giving a nickel here and a dime there and taking care of those less fortunate than ourselves are ways we obtain some positive recall of our external "I"s that will tide us over the times when our intellectual "I"s are undergoing a little bit of "self" doubt,.

To have the wherewithal to indulge ourselves, give up private possessions in exchange for a manufactured picture of our external "I"s that stabilizes our intellectual "I"s when we are cast in doubt, to be able to buy self-esteem, requires prosperity.

And, as we saw in Chapter Seven, the effect of prosperity on recall is the evolution of the ubiquitous "I" from one informed by Golden Rule Behavior to one informed by Exalted Empathy.

The nine percent of society that are close to the trade routes and thus the most prosperous, cluster in the consensual coteries around which the ubiquitous "I" informed by Exalted Empathy evolves.

Once prosperity evolves Exalted Empathy in the nine percent, Exalted Empathy controls the direction society takes. Therefore, while the ninety percent remains influenced largely by a ubiquitous "I" informed by Golden Rule Behavior, the nine percent are in control of society.

When we as members of society have to work hard to satisfy our basic need for food and shelter, all of our recall is used up forming pictures of the acts required to build and maintain shelter and harvest crops or bag game. The resulting food, a direct product of work, is shared in accordance with our concentric circles of recall so that those less fortunate, the young, the old and others that cannot provide for themselves, are taken care of by relatives or friends.

When a society produces more food and shelter than it consumes, then it begins to prosper. Not all people that can work have to work, and recall is freed up to dwell on how to better do the work or how to produce more wants and thus more paths to prosperity. Freeing up recall creates complexity, technological innovation.

We are then faced with an escalating spiral in which the more prosperous we become, the more free time we have to manufacture recall. The more time we have to manufacture recall, the more time we have to recall those less fortunate than ourselves.

And, with more prosperity, we have more, and in comparison, others have less, producing more people who are less fortunate than ourselves.

At the same time, with our recall freed up by prosperity, we can form pictures of ourselves doing all sorts of things that we have been programmed not to do. As prosperity expands, more and more of us with time and more on our hands begin to engage in prohibited behavior and, as violations of Golden Rule Behavior become widespread, the violations cease to produce neuronic impacts. Women smoke, lovers move in together, men leave potential spouses when they become pregnant, unwed mother raise children, married women get divorced.

Public fornication is still frowned upon but privately viewing fornication becomes public sport.

All of society's prohibitions, adopted when survival was dear and thus designed to prevent conflicts among its members, cease to be prohibitions when society becomes complex and prosperous.

Prosperity eases all conflicts.

With violations of Golden Rule Behavior common, punishment for violations becomes impracticable. Without punishment, violations that define Golden Rule Behavior do not produce neuronic impacts, and without neuronic impacts, cease to be moral violations.

However, the ubiquitous "I" still exists, society still demands some sort of objective standard of behavior, and to the extent that it doesn't, we, ourselves, need some sort of standard to provide guidance for the actions of our external "I"s in physical reality. If we don't have any guidance as to how our external "I"s should act, then we will either fly off the handle, take advantage of all the choices available and burn ourselves out or we will sink into inactivity because we will be unable to choose a proper course of conduct, and therefore be unable to act.

Our intellectual "I"s, in concert with the consensus, working through overlapping circles of consensual coteries begin to develop a philosophy that justifies all acts, anything is okay so long as it doesn't hurt anybody. The principle emerges that as long as we actually observe the golden rule, we won't have to worry about what is or is not Golden Rule Behavior.

We can pursue all pleasures so long as our pleasure does no harm to others.

It doesn't take a full generation, however, to realize that pleasure can't be stored in memory, it can only be experienced. There is no meaning in pleasure because, being a sensation rather than recall, there is nothing to compare! Like pain, only the circumstances of the pleasure and not the pleasure itself, is recallable. All the memory of pleasure does is drive us to recreate the circumstances in which we experienced the pleasure, usually an impossibility.

Without the prohibitions against violations that define Golden Rule Behavior, the conformity to which gave the appearance of meaning to our lives, and thus stability to our intellectual "I"s, with moral imperatives reduced to subjective determinations whether our pleasure is causing others harm, we find that our intellectual "I"s are left with no meaning for their existence.

Having no meaning for the existence of our intellectual "I"s produces massive neuronic impacts because we have to form pictures of our external "I"s acting in reality and with no meaning for the existence of our intellectual "I"s, the actions of our external "I"s, of our self, become meaningless.

We face death with a useless life, disappearing, like Alice's Cheshire cat, around a fading smile.

With the loss of Golden Rule Behavior to guide us, we have to find some other way to program the ubiquitous "I" so that we will have meaning at the core of our behavior. There is certainly nothing wrong with doing our own thing as long as we don't now *consciously* hurt anyone else, now "consciously" because after a generation of our good intentions being washed up on the shoals of reality, we have come to realize that we can never know the outcome of our actions and thus never know whether or not our actions will or will not hurt anyone.

However, we still need a standard that will give meaning to our actions and thus to our lives.

The standard is not hard to find, not only because we actually get pleasure out of helping others, thereby creating recall that compares our acts favorably with a societal ideal, but because the prosperity that is the product of technology is creating a lot of people who are less fortunate than ourselves, not only in our own society where we are becoming more prosperous, but in other societies, which are becoming poorer in comparison as we, the technologically adept society, emerge victor in the competition for the fruit on the limb, the world's resources.

What forms, then, is a ubiquitous "I" in which is placed the standards that measure our own self-worth by the extent to which we help those less fortunate than ourselves. Whenever our external "I"s are faced with a decision about which course of action to take, our intellectual "I"s consult the evolved ubiquitous "I" to determine if the course of conduct will cause us neuronic impacts. If taking away someone's benefits would produce neuronic impacts, while increasing them would eliminate neuronic impacts, our intellectual "I"s could not form a picture of our external "I"s taking part in eliminating benefits. We could only form a picture of our external "I"s increasing benefits, and thus any of our actual acts in physical reality will go to increase benefits.

If anyone attempts to take away the benefits of those less fortunate, the conflict becomes religious in nature, conflicting with the vary core of our being, the ubiquitous "I", and we respond with religious fervor.

The benefits of those less fortunate than ourselves become the very core of our intellectual "I"s because the acts we take in giving or preserving benefits to others become the recall that stabilizes our intellectual "I"s and produces purpose for our existence, thus giving our lives meaning.

We will do anything to maintain our good opinion of ourselves in order that we can continue to act positively in physical reality, and thus will condone any attack on those that attempt to destroy that good opinion. Because our good opinion is based on our charity to others, we are driven to destroy those who would take away the benefits we are providing to those less fortunate than ourselves.

However, benefits cost money.

The people in the society whose recall has been freed up by prosperity are not the people that are working to provide the members of society with the material goods that satisfy their wants.

When we aren't employed in work around the flow of goods and services from their source to their consumption, when we aren't employed around the trade routes that underlie commerce, we don't have access to the steady income that the flow of goods and services produces. We have to rely on spouses, parents, children or the good will of friends to satisfy our wants so that we can use our recall to improve the lot of those less fortunate than ourselves.

If we are not producing wealth, we don't have the coins we need to dump in the Styrofoam plastic cups of those less fortunate in order to maintain the favorable picture of our intellectual "I"s we need to act positively in reality.

We therefore have to pick someone else's pocket to get the coins needed to maintain our positive intellectual "I"s.

The only pockets we can pick are the pockets with coins, the pockets of those employed around the flow of goods and services that make up the trade that produces the wealth.

Pocket picking is stealing, the taking of private property the prohibition against which provides the basis of Golden Rule Behavior!

We thus have to violate the basic rule of society, the need to preserve private property against its taking by others, to get the coins we need to give to those less fortunate than ourselves. Because we are at the top of society, we are the sons and daughters of the trade lords, because we are the dominant consensual coterie that defines the standard of behavior for society, after all, we scorn Golden Rule Behavior in pursuit of the pleasures of its violations, because we make the rules, we can do away with the rules against taking and simply take.

We are driven to do this because to not do it, to not take care of those less fortunate than ourselves is to produce a picture of ourselves that opposes our intellectual "I"s, a picture that doesn't agree with the evolving ubiquitous "I" and, worse, removes all meaning from our lives.

What are we, after all, if we can't give back a little of what we have been blessed with?

What are we, after all, if, when we die, we can't say: "I have left the world a little better place?"

In a society in which the ubiquitous "I" dictates Golden Rule Behavior, the beggar who, instead of holding his hand outstretched, palm up, raised his fist in anger and demanded that his lot be improved, would be lucky to be ignored, with authority probably coming along and cutting off his fist. The farmer, who's probably feeding the beggar either willingly in the light of day or unwillingly in the middle of the night, demanding that authority feed the beggar, would also be ignored.

But let the daughter of a trade lord demand that the traders give the beggar some corn and she might gain an ear.

The relative pain the beggar produces in society is a measure of society's progress toward self-destruction. If nobody has any time to contemplate anything, with everyone engaged in doing the work that results in full bellies, the beggar is going to be an extra belly, and unless he has some ties to the community that puts him inside someone's concentric circles of recall, he is going to be in the way. In a society ruled by need, those that can't produce are in the way and will fall by the wayside, probably by running afoul of prohibitions against violations of Golden Rule Behavior, stealing another's property, the farmer's food.

With prosperity, an almshouse might be established by the religious authorities, but prosperity is driven by technology and produces more people less fortunate and society once again produces beggars, not just sitting by the trade routes, but clogging them

When the trade lord's daughter first notices the beggars, she is going to put her external "I" in the horrid conditions she perceives the beggar to be in, and she will receive neuronic impacts. Her father and her brother, both knee-deep in the daily activities of their businesses, are not going to have time to produce recall of the beggar, and even if they did, they are not going to receive neuronic impacts from picturing the beggar's condition, and even if they do, the neuronic impacts that the thought of making the beggar an indirect employee by supporting him out of the proceeds of the business would be more than sufficient to eliminate the picture from recall.

The beggar is not a source of neuronic impacts for the people engaged in trade because their recall is occupied with producing the wealth.

But the beggar is an incessant source of neuronic impacts for the trade lord's daughter. When she gets up, she recalls the beggar and feels her stomach tighten, her heart race, her skin grow clammy. She steals some food out of the pantry and takes it to a beggar, but it doesn't assuage her pain. She is driven, driven, I tell you, driven, to improve the lot of those less fortunate than herself. She mistakes the neuronic impacts she receives from perceiving the beggar in a degraded state for sexual excitement, romanticizes the beggar and uses words to turn the beggar into a Robin Hood for her children and those she wishes to enlist in her cause.

She hasn't anything else to do, any other way to justify her existence, produce the positive picture she needs to validate her intellectual "I", her self.

And because she is in the inner concentric circles of the recall of the prosperous, she has the awareness of the nine percent, the awareness that things can be changed, that a society that makes laws can change those laws.

She has, as is said of the initiate to the inner circles of prosperous authority, had her consciousness raised.

She may drive her father crazy enough to support her while she cavorts at the legislature, and she might drive her husband crazy enough to support the legislation she has produced that would require traders to feed the beggars, now legally classified as "those less fortunate" lest they be made to feel uncomfortable at being helped, and she would most certainly raise her children in the belief that traders should feed, cloth and provide telephones and television sets to those less fortunate, and she would be driven to her very death bed by neuronic impacts to get her laws passed, and the laws will be passed because as prosperity expands, Exalted Empathy expands and there can no argument against helping those less fortunate.

Those driven by Exalted Empathy have no awareness of the limitations of physical reality, or that wealth can only be created by work, making the outcome inescapable!

A society can not create an expanding circle of wants and the expectations that those wants will be satisfied in a world in which physical reality limits the satisfaction of those wants without heading down the path to self-destruction.

While the actions to raise those less fortunate is a liberal assault by those grouped around the wealth society produces, the inevitable success of the assault of Exalted Empathy on society engineered by prosperity creates a society where present resources are pledged for future benefits, a society in which benefits are overcommitted.

A society in which benefits are overcommitted is a conservative society because removing benefits is viewed as a taking in violation of the Golden Rule Behavior that holds society together.

Empathy is the process of creating a picture of our external "I"s under the conditions we see being experienced by others in physical reality. We have no idea whether the conditions we see others experiencing are causing them neuronic impacts, pain, but we know darn well that the conditions would cause us neuronic impacts, pain, because we experience neuronic impacts, pain, just by recalling our external "I"s being subjected to those conditions.

When we attempt to do things that will remove others from the conditions that cause us pain when we visualize our external "I"s experiencing the same conditions, we are engaging in Exalted Empathy, we are making ourselves feel good by doing things for those we feel are less fortunate than ourselves, and we are driven to do so by the neuronic impacts the original empathy produces.

Because we are not engaged in the trade activities that produce the wealth, the prosperity that produces the time that allows us to sit around and pursue Exalted Empathy, we have to get the funding to support our largess elsewhere.

The only source of funding is trade.

We therefore have to put a tax on the trade to carry out the activities that relieve our neuronic impacts.

However, because there is no limitation on wants which quickly become needs as the pain from neuronic impacts drives us to create recall of our wants as necessities for ourselves and therefore for others, and as there is a physical limitation to the wealth, the prosperity produced by trade, those engaged in trade resist such a tax and thus oppose our attempts to relieve the needs of others.

Any attempt to oppose doing those things which relieve our profound neuronic impacts, the pain that arises from opposing our core beliefs, results in even stronger neuronic impacts. When we are prevented from moving freely in physical reality, the neuronic impacts we receive produce feedback that causes us to form pictures of ourselves in recall removing the source of our pain. We focus on the source of the opposition to our taxes, those organized around the trade routes, and we vent the product of our pain, our anger and our frustration on them.

Of course, these are the very people whose work efforts are producing the prosperity that allows us to practice Exalted Empathy, but we don't have any recall dealing with producing wealth so we know nothing about the limitations of wealth, the fact that for wealth to flow, the infrastructure that provides it has to be maintained, that maintaining that infrastructure is a full time and exceedingly costly job, that taxing trade is not a removal of money from the pockets of those organized around trade, we are, after all their sisters and brothers, sons and daughters, rather a robbing of our children and grandchildren by taxing the infrastructure that produces future wealth.

But then, we aren't the first to bite the hand that feeds us!

We have no way to be aware of what is not in our recall, and the ignorance of the source of our wealth, the direct result of the complexity of the institutions that grow up to ensure that wealth moves from its source to its consumption in an efficient and orderly fashion, blinds us to the outcome of the acts we are driven to take with respect to that wealth.

Without recall of the problems involved in producing wealth, and only recall dealing with actions we believe will eliminate the neuronic impacts we imagine to be occurring in others because placing our external "I"s in the circumstances of others causes us pain, we forge ahead to our own destruction, delirious in the pleasure of our altruistic behavior which matches the societal ideal we now hold.

We can only speculate whether, without the catastrophic fracturing of society into many isolated societies that occurred on this particular planet, a single planet-wide society would have evolved which, through the lessons of countless interactions, recognized its need to balance the wants produced by unlimited recall with the limitations of physical reality.

But we don't live on a planet where wants are balanced by resources, and like the businessman whose dwindling resources, his customers, no longer support his plant, the assets producing his income, is forced to stick his fingers in the till to filch the cash flow, robbing the future to survive the present, having committed resources that don't exist to care for the future of those less fortunate has destroyed our future as well as the future of those less fortunate because we have to destroy the source of our prosperity to meet societal commitments.

The only segment of society that can object to helping those less fortunate is the segment that has to foot the bill, the group producing the wealth, and that group can not long object to having more in the face of the insistent demands of Exalted Empathy on behalf of those less fortunate.

Plotting this path to self-destruction is fairly easy.

The emergence of Golden Rule Behavior produces morality because violations of Golden Rule Behavior carry clearly defined punishments. Morality is behavior that is defined by punishment, either by the religious authorities who are empowered to consign souls to hell, or by the civil authorities who are able to take physical bodies and pretty much do with them as they please.

We consider ourselves higher life forms because we can distinguish between good and evil and thus can know the consequences of our actions.

The only way that we can know the consequences of our actions, however, is by comparing them with the ubiquitous "I" programmed into our recall by society so that we have recall that can produce a picture of our external "I"s being punished in accordance with our transgressions.

The only way we can provide meaning to our lives is to have a standard of conduct against which we can measure our actions.

When we make behavior relative, when we see acts for what they are, matter interacting with matter, and realize that acts in and of themselves have no meaning, we remove the value the restrictions on our acts produces even though it is the prohibition of acts by the threat of punishment that allows society to exist.

When the prohibitions against acting are made relative, when Golden Rule Behavior is tempered by the universal, "so long as it doesn't hurt anyone," then the determination of Golden Rule Behavior becomes subjective, and the objective standards that are required to hold society together are lost.

We no longer have any way to know what the consequences of our actions will be.

This is why there are absolute behavioral prohibitions. Behavioral prohibitions don't exist because someone sat down and thought them up, or because the heavens opened up and produced them in a religious revelation.

Behavioral prohibitions exist because it is the only way that society can exist!

The only way we can live together with minds that are structured the way our minds evolved is if we have prohibited acts because it is only by prohibiting violations of Golden Rule Behavior that we can know with any certainty the consequences of our actions. When we remove the programming of the ubiquitous "I" against violations of Golden Rule Behavior, and the certainty of the punishments that follow the violations, and when we reduce punishments for any acts that remain, for there are certainly still acts that shock the conscious, to rehabilitation because we cannot bear to form a picture of our external "I"s experiencing punishment, we are not freeing ourselves from the pain that is produced by living together in a society, we are increasing that pain.

Without any programming to inform our intellectual "I"s, we evolve Exalted Empathy as the only meaningful template for our behavior. But we have no way of knowing what the consequences of the acts we take to satisfy ourselves in our search for Exalted Empathy will be.

The pleasure the Exalted Empathy produces is consequence enough for us.

And there is no meaning in pleasure!

The damage that we wreak on the objects of our Exalted Empathy is catastrophic, but that is no bar to additional attempts, equally as catastrophic, because we are not attempting to improve the lot of those less fortunate than ourselves, we are simply attempting to produce Exalted Empathy that can block the increasing conflict between the expressed intentions of our acts and their obvious results, a conflict which, if allowed to form in our minds, would eliminate the very meaning of the self that is producing the recall, casting our minds into unfathomable despair.

We become moral puritans with no morality but the munificence of our intentions. Lacking Golden Rule Behavior to provide meaningful standards against which we can measure our conduct, we create an ersatz standard floating on consensual discomforts dealing with comity, restricting speech that we feel hurts the feelings of others, punishing offenses by shunning and forced rehabilitation, and restricting the freedom of the disempowered, those beholden to our largess whose dependence on our munificence binds them to our will and our children, already bound to our will, whose every movement becomes a potential crime for themselves or for someone else.

Those less fortunate end up better off than ourselves because, with the consequences of their behavior clearly defined, they have a brake on their behavior, while, driven by neuronic impacts to improve the lot of those less fortunate and with no way to measure the consequences of our acts, we end up with neuronic impacts no matter what we do.

The pleasures of Golden Rule Behavior occur by not acting, by conformity, the pleasure resulting by the escape from the pain of neuronic impacts action would produce, while the pleasures of Exalted Empathy come with activity. With the goals of Exalted Empathy unattainable, everybody with everything, the pleasure of Exalted Empathy becomes pain as our acts, instead of raising the level of those less fortunate, simply raises the number of those less fortunate!

On this particular planet, technology, and the resultant prosperity developed in the Western culture. After several millennia of individual societies within the western tradition reaching a resource wall and being forced to march out in legions to take over the resources of other societies, resulting in a recorded history devoted almost entirely to bloodshed, a point has been reached in which one of those societies, the globally oriented admixture of individual societies that make up the United States, has obtained the technological capability, and the wealth, to dominant the globe and realize what was lost when society was fractured asunder, a single society in which resources match wants, bringing the capability of survival once again within reach.

However, to preserve its wealth and satisfy its commitments to its own members, and in making commitments to members of other societies in response to the Exalted Empathy which views members of other societies as those less fortunate, the United States and its trading partners have to maintain its trade routes on an offensive basis, dictating commercial terms that are disadvantageous to the very people it considers to be those less fortunate.

The question then becomes, will Exalted Empathy drive us to loot the world in the name of charity, or will some intervening force be able to bring the wants of an emerging world society into line with available resources.

13.   THE PATH TO SELF-DESTRUCTION

During the nineteen fifties, anti-communists were fond of saying that communism couldn't stand because its demand that all share equally was against human nature. No one knew what the nature of human nature was, but we have a long history of human behavior, and humans have long since demonstrated the importance of private property. Private property represents food, shelter and safety and the history of human behavior is essentially a history of protecting what we have from others who would steal our resources to fill their belies and, when necessary, taking from others to fill our own bellies.

The altruism at the center of the communist conflict did not arise from poverty, but rather from prosperity.

Altruism doesn't turn poverty into prosperity, it turns prosperity into poverty!

A myth has grown up, primarily as a result of the Darwinian conceit that we are descended from animals and thus all of our characteristics are animalistic, but also from misguided pride that drives us to distance ourselves from our animalistic behavior, that when we violate society's rules, engage in acts that violate Golden Rule Behavior, we are demonstrating our animalistic roots, but when we create, we are displaying some sort of spiritual, godlike characteristic beyond human ken which allows us to enter a plane above human striving, and that our creations, our art and literature and music save us from our animalistic roots.

The fact is, we are, as are all animals, a compilation of evolved characteristics put together in a manner best capable of dealing with our environment. Because we are the most complex of evolved organisms with the widest variety of interacting characteristics, we have the best chance of extending our range of survivability in physical reality, and thus developing additional characteristics that might be inherited by our biological descendants or by some other compilation of characteristics that replaces us.

That doesn't mean we don't share characteristics with animals. The monkey that uses the most convenient tool to scoop up its food is doing nothing more than matching reality with recall, and the dog that viciously attacks another dog that is trying to take its bone is doing nothing more than trying to maintain the picture of reality it has in recall, a picture of its external "I" chewing on the bone.

We have, however, unlike all other matter, animate or inanimate, ambulatory or nonambulatory, evolved characteristics that desensitize our subsystems to the extent that we can form a picture in our recall and maintain that picture even though the picture, not existing in reality, would normally cause us to immediately attempt to make the picture a reality or abandon the act the picture represents, eliminate it completely in the face of the pain, the neuronic impacts, the resulting conflict produced.

Instead of just reacting to reality, we can contemplate our acts in relation to reality.

Because we can hold a picture in recall which has no counterpart in reality, we can alter the current levels of the individual elements of the picture and thus create a picture of reality that does not exist in reality.

However, when we create realities in recall that totally oppose the reality on which we are concentrating, our subsystems are not so desensitized that we do not become uncomfortable. As we view reality with our recall, when we have a picture of reality that doesn't exist in reality firmly in recall, our desensitized subsystems do not protect us from the resulting neuronic impacts and we are driven to go out and change reality so that it matches our recall.

But the basic operation of our mind doesn't differ much from any other mind that evolved to move animate matter through physical reality because there is only one way a detector, the mind, can accomplish such a task, and that is by matching reality with recall.

The altruism that underlies communism, to all according to their needs, is an idealized statement of the ubiquitous "I" as informed by Exalted Empathy, an evolutionary product of prosperity. However, while our minds were focused on whether communism would either solve the problem of universalizing Exalted Empathy to produce a society in which all shared equally or collapse in the heap of private interests that were sure to be broiling beneath its surface, the possibility that communism might actually have been used as a cover for one dog taking the bone of another dog, the natural outcome of a struggle for control of trade routes, a strategy by one of the fragmented societies on this particular planet to wrest control of the trade routes from another fragmented society, the society that ran those trade routes, has been obscured.

Whether communism was a home grown effort springing from the desire of a people to be free from despotism or a germinated horror designed to eliminate competitors from the playing field, what communism actually accomplished was the destruction of one trading empire, the British Empire and the transfer and consolidation of the control of its trade routes to another trading empire, the American globally oriented process of consolidating the diverse cultures that have grown up in the millennia since the catastrophic occurrence that fractured them.

The term "human nature", embodied in the struggle of art and literature and music to overcome bestiality, disguises the real question of behavior that results from the basic fact that we are animate matter that merely responds to the conflicts produced by the operation of the detector that is the mind when reality and recall disagree.

Our minds produce pain.

We seek to avoid the pain.

That's how the world works.

The mind is a system that allows us to respond to conflicts and therefore allows us to move through physical reality.

But, because of the by-product of the mind's operation, its ability to produce recall that doesn't exist in reality, our behavior, human behavior, is something more.

Human behavior exists apart from the behavior of all other animate matter because we can alter our environment to extend our range of survivability by becoming independent of that environment.

However, we have not spent our time using our ability to create a reality that doesn't exist in reality to extend our range of survivability in physical reality. We are not even aware that this is the way we must exploit the by-product of our mind's operation if we are to have a future.

Because our history fragmented our development into separate societies, we use the by-product of our mind's operation to recall provocations that are specific with respect to our fellow humans. While animals might well take a disliking against a specific competitor, an animal's recall simply keeps it away from other predators as classes rather than as individuals. While our dog might well despise the next door neighbor's dog, and will fight him at the drop of a hat, he doesn't daydream about crafting instruments that could be used to pull the nails slowly out of his competitor's foot.

We alone have the ability to alter our recall and therefore create a reality that would not otherwise exist, are in fact driven to create that reality by the neuronic impacts that drive us to build castles in the sky, take preemptive revenge on our competitors or just destroy those who have caused us pain.

Because our recall is unlimited and thus the acts that we can take in reality are unlimited, we have to make agreements as to what behavior is acceptable. All who view the castles aspiring to the sky will honor the recall that produced the castle. All who review the results of revenge will avoid forming pictures of the revenge because the neuronic impacts that results from the unpleasant recall make the recall distasteful.

We learn to classify behavior by neuronic impacts, the pain the behavior produces.

As long as we don't have recall of the bleaching bones and agonizing cries of the labor that built the spires when we espy the spires, we will be ennobled by the spires.

Human behavior is the result of the reaction of individuals to the neuronic impacts that flow from the necessary interactions of individuals and because neuronic impacts cause pain, and the normal reaction to pain is to respond with pain, the institution that the necessary interactions create, society, has to in turn create institutions that will moderate human behavior so that the individuals within the society can continue to operate as a society, continue to receive the physical benefits of society, the benefits of having their bellies full, their bodies sheltered from the cold and a safe place to raise their young.

Technology, and the prosperity technology produces, drastically alters the relationship of society to the individual, creating classes of individuals with different levels of awareness and different levels of participation in the benefits of society. Because technology replaces cooperative labor to common ends and reduces the number of people it takes to fill everyone's bellies, ways have to be devised to allow participation in the fruits of society by noncontributors.

Assuming that society had not been fractured by some unfathomable catastrophe and thus had not grown up with the necessity of utilizing technology to protect trade routes, directing its development toward conflict, war and death, society over a period of time, as a result of the pressures of population on resources, would probably have developed an orderly process of limiting population so that technology could move available goods and services to its members without raising resource allocation problems or creating a class without ready access to goods and services.

But that's not the way it happened!

The technology that did develop, designed to conform directly to the operation of the mind, preserve and protect, destroy and take, has served to mask the reality of limited resources by eliminating large segments of the populations competing for those resources from benefiting from the resources or by eliminating large segments of the population competing for those resources altogether. And, now, offering absolutely no respect for those that forcefully and endlessly argue that there are no limits to growth, a belief held firmly in the recall of significant segments of society, segments that avoid facing reality by creating recall that gives reign to the unlimited exercise of Exalted Empathy, resources are limited and there are limitations to growth because there is no limitation on the ability of recall to produce wants and an absolute limitation on the ability of physical reality to satisfy those wants.

The belief that we can produce technology in an ever aspiring arc that will accommodate as many people as those people can produce is merely a belief placed in recall to avoid the stark fact that there are always more people than there are resources, if there weren't, there would be no poverty, and the additional fact that an expanding population in a technological society is actually synonymous with poverty.

Making up beliefs to protect ourselves from neuronic impacts is a necessity to eliminate the neuronic impacts for things such as falling objects where we simply haven't been able to comprehend or for visions such as the end of the human race where we simply can not force ourselves to comprehend.

And make no mistake, the end of the human race is what we are talking about!

Because we have directed our efforts to creating technologies to deal with our immediate concerns, the weapons that would give us trade dominance, we have spent our mental energy producing things that work in reality and ignored the reasons why those things actually work in reality. We create rockets that can travel across the face of the globe striking targets on the opposite side of the planet ten to fifteen thousand miles away, and we haven't the foggiest idea about the nature of the fire that pushes those rockets, we don't even have general terms to express what is going on when something burns, modifying technical words like combustion into combusts or waxing poetic, the candle's lit. We load these rockets up with precise amounts of fuel so that they can stay in the air in spite of the attractive force and we don't have the foggiest idea how this force is generated, how it moves from one place to another or how it acts on matter so that the matter is moved back toward the source of the force, the nature of which we are also ignorant.

Because our ability to develop the technologies that extend our range of survivability in physical reality results from our ability to form pictures of a reality in our recall that doesn't exist in reality, we can just as well create reality about the basis of technology in recall that has no relationship at all to physical reality. When we send a rocket on its way, we believe that the mechanical operation of what we have engineered in reality proves everything we have made up about that reality. We think that our concepts of force are proven because we can combine chemicals that push our rockets with predictable effect and that we comprehend the structure of matter because we can blow up the bombs that are on the tops of those rockets with mind boggling results.

We think we know things when we know nothing about the most basic things in our existence, force and motion, what makes dropped objects fall and what makes the sun come up in the morning!

Because the technology we produce involves the alteration of physical reality to our benefit, if we want to alter physical reality to our benefit, it is absolutely necessary for us to produce accurate pictures of physical reality in our recall. If we think we know something about physical reality and we don't, then we don't have an accurate picture of physical reality upon which to base alternatives in our recall. If we make up facts that don't exist in physical reality, mass/gravity, light waves, moving charges, molecular magnets, swirling masses of gas, then we have not only produced an inaccurate picture of physical reality, we have produced a distorted picture of physical reality.

If we produce a distorted picture of physical reality, then the efforts we go to in our recall to change that picture in order to change physical reality will be for naught. If we eliminate the obstacles in our existence by assuming away their existence, rule mass to be a property of matter that distorts empty space to effect other matter, claim planets move because of historic forces or believe that light is like a water wave with no existence independent of a nonexistent medium, we will simply never attempt to produce a recall that can be modified to take advantage of their existence, for exist they do.

When we produce a distorted picture of physical reality, we will produce an inaccurate technology, and to the extent that our technology is inaccurate, is not aligned with physical reality, we will not be able to modify physical reality to our advantage, modify it to effectively extend our range of survivability into the future.

Instead, we will use our recall to produce toys which in turn produce more wants which in turn produce more poverty!

The cycle of destruction that the increased wants created by the prosperity inaccurate technology produces is clear.

The mind's process of producing a picture of the external "I" in order to move animate matter through physical reality, when evolved to the point that the mind can hold pictures of physical reality in recall when physical reality does not exist, will always allow the production of a picture of the external "I" in physical reality without the goods and services presently possessed because there will always be examples in physical reality of people without the possessions.

As wealth increases, and as the size of the poverty class increases either in reality or in comparison, neuronic impacts will drive society to distribute wealth among all members of society as the Exalted Empathy of the ubiquitous "I" replaces the former Golden Rule Behavior of the ubiquitous "I" in the prosperous group at the top of society.

There is no way around it!

Helping those less fortunate is the result of the mind's operation, and because the mind's operation produces pain, the human behavior the mind produces is human behavior that seeks to eliminate the pain.

We will simply not do things that will cause ourselves pain. We may even know what the future holds, that what we are doing is going to lead to our own self-destruction, but we simply cannot stop our behavior because our behavior drives us to avoid the pain of creating pictures of our external "I"s refusing to help the outstretched hand of those less fortunate than ourselves, or producing a picture of our external "I"s dying never having improved the lot of others in physical reality, of not giving back, of creating a picture of our external "I"s dying without a life that we view as meaningful.

When iron metallurgy replaced bronze as a source of weapons technology in the Mediterranean area, the bronze age came to an end. Bronze is an alloy of tin and copper, and the only tin deposits that existed were in the Americas. The trade in bronze created large pools of wealth which had their source in the tin mines of the "netherlands", the place where, to the people of the Mediterranean, the sun came from in the morning and went at night. Wealthy cities and populations grew up in the Americas during the bronze age and these civilizations were isolated when the need for trading tin as bronze ceased.

These civilizations, the remnants of which we have but whispers, and the reality of which we have specific records dealing with the Incas in South America and the Aztecs in North America, occupied tropical climates that were the source of considerable food wealth and minimal need for shelter.

With bronze age prosperity, and a ruling class informed by Exalted Empathy, these societies contained well defined class structures which, as expanding populations increased pressures on the food resources, drove food production to the limit of the land.

The principle that trade will brook no behavior that will cause its interruption is based on the fact that the people the trade is benefiting have in their recall, in the very center of their picture of self, recall that shows them possessing the fruits of the trade and that any picture that shows them without the fruits of that trade will produce neuronic impacts that far outweigh any neuronic impacts produced by violating Golden Rule Behavior.

We will murder in wars, take the possessions of others, and willingly rape the land and all its occupants to preserve our trade routes.

The ubiquitous "I" using Exalted Empathy as its template can place a burden on trade by direct taxes or regulation, retarding the movement of goods and services from their source to consumption, simply because the intellectual "I"s informed by Exalted Empathy have no way to draw a connection between the trade, the production of wealth, and the wealth needed to answer the call of the ubiquitous "I" to help those less fortunate.

But without question, when the belly starts to growl, the connection between the burden on trade and the trade's production of wealth, of food, becomes apparent. When communism fell and food became scarce in the Soviet Union, engineered equality came to an abrupt end as the strong, men, forced women out of the few paying jobs that were left and the rapacious shoveled all competition that showed even a hint of weakness into frosty graves.

The neuronic impacts produced by the recall forced into the mind by hunger has no peer. It controls the pictures our intellectual "I"s create of our external "I"s and the ubiquitous "I" be damned, at least until the stomach is full.

With civilizations isolated in the Americas by the collapse of the Bronze Age in the face of iron smelting technology in the Mediterranean, *much as we have, by our inaccurate technology, isolated ourselves on this planet,* population growth began to eat into the available food supply and shortages began to affect the nine percent of the ninety, nine and one directly by scarcity, or indirectly by increasing the visibility of those less fortunate.

Although we can only puzzle over the ashes today, an empire in the Americas would have consolidated by gradually removing competitive societies and thus eliminating the source of plunder needed to satisfy the growing wants of its expanding population. Physically affected by an overextended population and with no rivals from which to steal, with no way to deny the demands of the remaining ninety percent and no ability to punish transgressions because Exalted Empathy always considers those deserving of punishment as less fortunate, the operation of the mind dictated courses of action over which the nine percent had no control.

To take our self-worth solely on the basis of helping those less fortunate than ourselves and then be put in a position of being surrounded by those less fortunate with no ability to take action that gives the appearance of helping those less fortunate has to be unbearable.

But to face, at the same time, the constant threat of actually starving to death, not empathetically starving to death, but rib thrusting, face sunken actually starving to death, becomes insupportable.

Picturing our external "I"s no longer existing will drive us to take any action!

With the collapse of the trade routes to the Mediterranean, the elite in the isolated empires of the Americas found themselves experiencing the most painful neuronic impacts possible, the paralyzing neuronic impacts that we interpret as fear.

These neuronic impacts drive the production of recall that will eliminate the neuronic impacts, recall that produces pictures of our external "I"s taking any action necessary to eliminate the pain.

What form would these pictures take in an isolated society whose needs had evolved beyond the capacity of its remaining resources?

The cause of the pain is the fear of starving.

The fear of starving is sourced in too many people and not enough food.

There was in the Americas no way to increase the food supply, that course had been exhausted over the centuries either by applying technological improvements to farming or by taking the fruit from the limbs of the trees of others.

The only remaining course of action to eliminate the pain would be to eliminate the people whose existence was causing the pain!

The nine percent that are responsible for taking care of the ninety percent, driven by neuronic impacts to help those less fortunate and unable to use technology to do so and faced with dwindling food supplies, were forced to act and the only act left to them was to reduce the number of stomachs trying to belly up to the trough.

When faced with a resource wall, the nine percent are going to be driven to do the same thing they do when societal resources are threatened by external taking, they are going to abdicate their authority to the one percent that don't experience neuronic impacts, those in society who have escaped society's programming, who don't have a ubiquitous "I" that would prevent them from forming plans of action leading to the elimination of those less fortunate than themselves.

These are not conscious decisions on the part of the ninety, nine or one percent of society, but an expression of the societal determination to maintain itself.

The one percent of society that have escaped programming and thus are informed by neither the Exalted Empathy of the nine percent nor the Golden Rule Behavior of the ninety percent, rise to the top of society when society is threatened from the outside by those wanting to take its resources, or when society, threatened from inside by an expanding population with expanding wants facing limited resource has to organize itself to take the resources of other societies.

In the Americas after the collapse of the Bronze Age, the trade routes exporting tin dried up. Like China's tea sucked silver out of the British Empire in the nineteenth century, the export of tin from the Americas had sucked gold extracted from South African mines out of the Mediterranean coffers, gold that was plentiful in the America after their rediscovery millennia later.

Just as the British Empire had sought to stem the outflow of silver to China by exporting opium, so too had the Mediterranean bronze consumers sought to stabilize the outflow of gold by exporting grain as return cargo for the ships transporting the bronze to the Mediterranean.

As with all prosperous populations that expand to the level of the available food supply, the prosperous societies of the Americas expanded beyond the ability of the land to support them, the imported grain becoming a necessity.

Whatever percentage of the food supply the holds of the Bronze Age vessels provided the Americas as return cargo, the percentage became zero as the ability of iron to cut through bronze like butter — the proverbial Gordian knot of iron smelting being sliced by Alexander the Great's steel sword — dried up the trade routes, putting pressure on the societies that had grown up around the trading centers and the mines to reach out and take their neighbor's resources, allowing the one percent to rise to the top and take control.

This one percent, unencumbered by the delusions that the ubiquitous "I" places in recall would have clearly seen the resulting clashes as clashes over resources, that for each of their societies to survive, it would have to devote its resources to taking the resources of other societies.

Taking another's resources, however, violates the Golden Rule Behavior that holds society together and is distasteful to the Exalted Empathy that governs the recall of the prosperous elements of the society, the nine percent.

The one percent therefore had to put their societies on a war footing, producing recall that would replace the recall that controlled behavior, the ubiquitous "I" informed by Exalted Empathy in the case of the nine percent and the ubiquitous "I" informed by Golden Rule Behavior in the case of the ninety percent.

Whatever recall the one percent created to occupy the recall of a society increasingly devoted to taking to survive, incessant strife over succeeding generations would produce a consensus reality dealing with that recall and would, in effect, produce a new ubiquitous "I" that informed the intellectual "I"s of both the nine percent and the ninety percent.

This ubiquitous "I" would embody self-sacrifice as an ideal because it was only by dying in the effort to preserve and protect or destroy and take, that society could survive.

Intellectual "I"s informed by a ubiquitous "I" that embodied self-sacrifice are intellectual "I"s willing to cast their external "I"s on the spears of the enemy in order to preserve society, and therefore maintain those in their inner concentric circles of recall with food, shelter and safety.

Meaning to an intellectual "I" whose ubiquitous "I" is informed by self-sacrifice would then be found in the act of self-sacrifice.

While the intellectual "I" informed by Golden Rule Behavior finds self-worth in dying having lived by the standard of conduct prescribed by society and the intellectual "I" informed by Exalted Empathy finds self-worth in dying having helped those less fortunate, having given something back, having left the world a little better place, the intellectual "I" informed by self-sacrifice finds self-worth in simply dying!

Under normal circumstances, as a society successfully aggregated the available resources and eliminated potential claimants to those resources, it would have to revert back to a standard of Golden Rule Behavior to hold itself together. However, with the isolated societies in the Americas consolidating into single dominant continental empires and with resources now limited, with no remaining societies available for the taking that is necessary to satisfy the needs and wants of the expanding population of the triumphant society, the resource limitation brings the problem of too many people with too few resources to the fore.

With the one percent still in control and with the existence of society still threatened, society exploits the ubiquitous "I" informed by self-sacrifice to protect itself.

And thus the sacrifices, found in such terrible abundance in the Andes of the Incas and the Mexico of the Aztecs at the time of the rediscovery of America, came about.

Priest castes were organized around religions that processed people like cattle in the name of staving off destruction

Contrary to myth, which paints a picture of the sacrifices being carried out on enemy soldiers as acts of revenge, bone fields disclose that the revenge carried out on enemy soldiers was not the bliss of opiates followed by the quick thrust of a knife, but rather the slow cracking of bones through any medium capable of being conceived by the recall of man.

The sacrifices were produced by population pressure on resources to take advantage of an ideal of behavior, sacrificing oneself so that others may feed, that developed from a ubiquitous

"I" that required the ultimate sacrifice to maintain the safety of society against all comers.

With sacrifice justified as necessary to control overpopulation, blood poured down the steps of the pyramids which, palaces of death in reality, were fountains of life in recall.

But not for long!

The basic glue that holds society together is Golden Rule Behavior. Golden Rule Behavior is an absolute necessity for individuals to come together and the only reason that individuals come together is that society better provides for their basic needs, the need for food, shelter and a safe place to raise their children.

A society that sanctions murder is sanctioning a violation of Golden Rule Behavior no matter what meaning society attempts to attach to it because murder deals with death, and death deals with existence, with the source of life, the basic question that drives the formation of society.

A society that, beguiled by prosperity, has allowed overpopulation to drive it to tolerate violations of Golden Rule Behavior ceases to provide a reason to continue as a society, fewer neuronic impacts than individuals would experience if they were on their own.

Witnessing continued violations of Golden Rule Behavior without those violations being redressed, with no punishment to produce standards against which a life can be measured, the neuronic impacts become greater than the neuronic impacts produced by a picture of the external "I" without the society, and so the members of a sacrificial society abandon the society, drift away into the jungle, and, without a reason for existence, the society dies, its ruins sinking under the rain forest, its memory a recall that, producing mild neuronic impacts, leaves a slight distaste in the mouth but little memory in the mind because we do not like to produce recall in our children that would cause them pain.

As we move toward a global economy with an international trading system on a planet fast becoming so overpopulated that its cities are teeming piles of poverty, we are facing the same problem.

We are driven by neuronic impacts to help those less fortunate than ourselves, but if we feed those less fortunate than ourselves, they reproduce to the level of food supplies and slightly beyond, worsening the conditions we attempt to alleviate.

Yet we cannot form pictures of our external "I"s not aiding the outstretched hand!

We are in a perilous situation, and how we approach the problem, how we deal with the neuronic impacts that drive us, how we abdicate action to solve our dilemma will determine whether we will be able to reknit the planet into a global society, or whether we will create a catastrophic consolidation that destroys us once again, fractures us once more, with this fracturing being the last, the end of the unique life form that evolved on this planet because, having screwed up the technology we developed and having little hope of recouping what we never had, and with time running out on a rapidly cooling planet, we will simply dissolve into warring fractions seeking control over dwindling food supplies as the planet grows cold in space and dies.

We have developed a unique process in an attempt to solve our dilemma, even if we are unaware of that dilemma and even if we only dimly perceive the process.

While the religious institutions attempt to regulate our personal behavior and the government attempts to regulate behavior of every conceivable type, starting off regulating trade issues and then regulating behavioral issues by attempting to control how we think, recreating the primitive connection between the civil and the religious, a third type of regulation has evolved to deal with the problems involved in consolidating the fractured cultures on the planet into a global society. The birth of this sector of society occurred when society became aware of the need to incorporate the vast fortunes with which technology endowed individual members of society into institutions that benefited society but remained outside governmental control.

Following the Rockefeller model of divesting trade fortunes from family control, it is generally recognized today that individuals who, through a mixture of personal characteristics and luck, amass fortunes beyond the needs of themselves or their descendants for many years to come, must devise those fortunes into the public sector to benefit the continued evolution of the public interest. This has resulted in the creation of the nonprofit sector, an evolution of the failed Old Boy's Club model that coordinated societal efforts under the defunct British Empire. The availability of these semi-public funds has spawned the vast foundation community and the associated public charities, the sprawling research facilities of colleges and universities, the special think tanks and private institutes, and the trade associations and labor organizations that operate outside of political or religious supervision but whose overriding goal is to accomplish what individuals driven by the ubiquitous "I" using Exalted Empathy as a template seek to accomplish, helping those less fortunate, *who, facing extinction, is all of us,* but doing so without being driven by the accompanying neuronic impacts, without the need to derive personal pleasure from altruistic activities.

The nonprofit community seeks to put altruism on an objective footing.

Separating efforts to improve the lot of those less fortunate from the need to do so that is driven by Exalted Empathy is important because, while no one can portend the effect of his or her actions, either individually or collectively, the coin we place in the outstretched hand might purchase the bullet used the next day to kill us, buffering the drive to help those less fortunate with an institution that is not itself subject to neuronic impacts, driven by considerations of self-worth nor under the governance of individuals who are motivated by religious, political, military or trade considerations increases the chance that actions will be taken for long term benefit rather than short term pleasure, raising the probability that the actions will be true to their mark.

Because trade routes are international and the financial markets that make trade possible are international, the fortunes that trade produces must flow into supranational, and thus suprasocietal institutions whose goals are to ease the world past national boundaries.

But, the people that staff the organizations that make up the institutions are the same people that society evolves, and these people, belonging to the nine percent of the ninety, nine and one that trade wealth educates and shapes, are also controlled by the dictates of the ubiquitous "I" using Exalted Empathy as a template.

The inescapable fact that society's institutions are operated by the individuals society produces, individuals informed by one of the then available ubiquitous "I"s societal interactions generate, raises the basic question we face in evolving into a single society.

Will the suprasocietal institutions we create be able to knit the world together before the Exalted Empathy of the nine percent gains control of the decision making process and turns consolidation into catastrophe!

Already, attempts to dampen rampant population growth, sterilization and prophylactic programs in countries with high growth rates, even when instituted in spite of local superstitions and vigilant religious authorities are attacked by third party elites who have no direct interest in the outcome, but do have an emotional interest based on the ubiquitous "I" dictating that such programs are racist or administered without the informed consent of the women affected, informed consent being a concept that belongs to the educated intellectual "I" rather than the external "I" in physical reality with ten kids hanging on ragged apron strings. To bolster their position, those driven by Exalted Empathy to intrude in the lives of those less fortunate than themselves even when those less fortunate than themselves are attempting to improve their own lot, partner with the other ninety percent of society still informed by a ubiquitous "I" adhering to Golden Rule Behavior who cry murder of the unborn.

Others, seeped in Exalted Empathy, see the fruits of free trade, the exportation of whole factories into cheap labor markets, as the exploitation of slave labor, and joining with shoemakers and seamstresses informed by Golden Rule Behavior who fear for their jobs organize boycotts of tennis shoes and underwear, and where that fails to obtain immediate redress for the wrongs perceived by placing their external "I"s in the foreign factories of their imagination, demand legislation to imprison the guardian of any child found wearing the offending shoes or shorts, and this without regard to the personal income stream that might prepare a factory worker's son or daughter for a career with the World Bank or the International Monetary Fund, and without regard to the reality that increasing income reduces population.

We are driven to interfere in the lives of those we label less fortunate than ourselves by neuronic impacts that will not be denied, and when the focus of those neuronic impacts becomes the suprasocietal institutions created to solve the ultimate problem, the problem of consolidating the world against encroaching population and poverty, then Exalted Empathy driven by the need to do personal charity is in danger of taking over the programs of the nonprofit sector, directing their course toward destruction — instead of controlling the demand on resources, demanding the redistribution of prosperity until all prosperity is eliminated.

If this occurs, if Exalted Empathy combines with Golden Rule Behavior to overcome objective efforts to create a world in which production has a reasonable chance over several generations of matching supportable consumption, then the elite, the nine of the ninety, nine and one whose benefits will be preserved at all costs, will simply step aside, open the doors to the jails of a million minds, the one percent, the psychopaths who, unfettered by restraints contained in ubiquitous "I"s shaped by either Golden Rule Behavior or Exalted Empathy against which to measure their acts, will roam the countryside, shaping the last society the Earth will ever know and bringing to a conclusion the genetic strain that evolved as life on this planet.